Level Land: Poems For and About the I35 Corridor

Level Land:
Poems For and About the I35 Corridor

Co-Edited by Crag Hill and Todd Fuller

ISBN: 978-1-942956-42-6
Library of Congress Control Number: 2022944669

Cover Design: Erin Simms
Typeset by Chelsea Frederick
Copyeditors: Justin Trahan and Kayla Umbenhaur

Lamar University Literary Press
Beaumont, Texas

DEDICATION

First, acknowledgements: Dr. Jonathan Stalling at the University of Oklahoma brought together the editors of this anthology, Crag Hill and Todd Fuller, in 2013, quite by design, since Stalling was managing the Mark Allen Everett Poetry Series and needed assistance running / curating the Series. He did so because Hill and Fuller expressed to Stalling both a love of poetry and a desire to be involved. We are thankful to Jonathan for his need to over-work, over-achieve, and over-friend, thereby making it possible for us to meet and begin a professional / collaborative relationship, which has evolved into much more.

Also, the Mark Allen Everett Poetry Series, and the members of the Mark Allen Everett Family Fund (and the Oklahoma City Community Foundation), generously provided funding for and believed in the I-35 project. Board member Nancy Yoch consistently gave sage guidance assisting us in our efforts to apply for annual renewal grants.

Sara Wilson was / has been tireless in her efforts to assist us in making this anthology emerge into existence. Without her good work, the initial processes would have taken much longer to complete.

Finally, we thank our families, whose encouragement, patience, and belief allowed us to work and endure.

Recent Poetry from Lamar University Literary Press

Bobby Aldridge, *An Affair of the Stilled Heart*
Walter Bargen, *My Other Mother's Red Mercedes*
Charles Behlen, *Failing Heaven*
Jerry Bradley, *Collapsing into Possibility*
Mark Busby, *Through Our Times*
Julie Chappell, *Mad Habits of a Life*
Stan Crawford, *Resisting Gravity*
Glover Davis, *My Cap of Darkness*
William Virgil Davis, *The Bones Poems*
Jeffrey DeLotto, *Voices Writ in Sand*
Chris Ellery, *Elder Tree*
Dede Fox, *On Wings of Silence*
Alan Gann, *That's Entertainment*
Larry Griffin, *Cedar Plums*
Michelle Hartman, *Irony and Irrelevance*
Katherine Hoerth, *Goddess Wears Cowboy Boots*
Michael Jennings, *Crossings: A Record of Travel*
Gretchen Johnson, *A Trip Through Downer, Minnesota*
Ulf Kirchdorfer, *Hamlet in Exhile*
Jim McGarrah, *A Balancing Act*
J. Pittman McGehee, *Nod of Knowing*
Erin Murphy, *Ancilla*
John Milkereit, *Drive the World in a Taxicab*
Laurence Musgrove, *Bluebonnet Sutras*
Benjamin Myers, *Black Sunday*
Janice Northerns, *Some Electric Hum*
Godspower Oboido, *Wandering Feet on Pebbled Shores*
Carol Coffee Reposa, *Underground Musicians*
Jan Seale, *Particulars*
Steven Schroeder, *the moon, not the finger, pointing*
Glen Sorestad, *Hazards of Eden*
Vincent Spina, *The Sumptuous Hills of Gulfport*
W.K. Stratton, *Betrayal Creek*
Wally Swist, *Invocation*
Ken Waldman, *Sports Page*
Loretta Diane Walker, *Ode to My Mother's Voice*
Dan Williams, *Past Purgatory, a Distant Paradise*
Jonas Zdanys, *Three White Horses*

For information on these and other Lamar University Literary
Press books go to www.Lamar.edu/literarypress

CONTENTS

103   Cross Timbers

181   Tall Grass Prairie

233   Upper Mississippi

INTRODUCTION

Terrestrial, Sub-surface, Surface, Aero-Ecologies:

When we first began thinking about I35, we discussed the interstate as a creative corridor—one used by writers, musicians, and other artists to get from one gig to the next—roads uniting us from one county to the next, one state to the next. We wondered aloud in a planning session, "what if we could create a network from one university / college / town to the next, so that writers could move from one place to the next in a seamless way?" This was 2014. The next year, in April, co-editor Crag Hill curated a month-long feature / anthology of poets who contributed to *Truck: I35 Creativity Corridor*. At the time, Hill wrote:

You'll be treated to poetry . . . to glimpses of people and places from the southern plains to the northern heartland, to snippets of the mapped spine of the U.S.

Inspired by [our] vision of a creativity corridor marked by I35 where commerce is art and literature, where political borders dissolve, where the land rises up in the spirit and the word, this project will drive you places you didn't know you wanted to be.

Initially, we conceived of the project as contained within the geo-political borders of the present-day United States. We discovered in 2016, however, the southern route extended into Mexico, and was, in fact, a long-time trade way predating euro-presence / occupation. Today, though I35 ends in Laredo, Texas, a few blocks north of the border, the road continues in Mexico as Federal Highway 85 and terminates in Mexico City. We also learned the northern U.S. terminus at Duluth continues to Thunder Bay, Ontario. Ernest Hemingway famously raved about the fishing in and around the area, specifically the rainbow trout. Because of this, we quickly moved to include Mexican and Canadian poets and make the first interstate anthology international.

From the outset, we were especially cognizant of Indigeneity—its layers and complexities touching the lands, peoples (tribal nations), cultures, ways of knowing and being, and histories and how they're told or remembered and by whom. We are keenly aware of historical narratives and their impact on the continent's Indigenous peoples. We're also mindful of the many imprint/s the first human inhabitants impressed upon / across the corridor, and we wanted to be both respectful and inclusive (celebratory, even) of frequently-neglected perspectives—especially in this space. After all, Indigenous peoples were the first observers, gazers, and architects / designers of the land and space over which I35 currently rests. Tribal nations / Indigenous peoples from the Zapotec, Aztec, Maya, and many more in present-day Mexico, to the Comanche, Wichita, Caddo, Kiowa Pawnee, Otoe-Missoria, Kaw, Osage, Omaha, Iowa, Lakota, and Ojibway (to name some, not all) in the present-day U.S., stewarded the lands, created agricultures, established arts, and developed towns, cultures, and civilizations.

So, we made a concerted effort to encourage Native poets with ties to the corridor to submit. A few of the Native poets you'll find include Kimberly Blaeser, Allison Adelle Hedge Coke, Laura Da', Sy Hoahwah, LeAnne Howe, Adrian Louis, Denise Low, Gus Palmer, Marcie Rendon, and C. R. Resetarits. There are more, and we hope you'll read the emerging Native authors with as much enthusiasm as those with whom you might be more familiar, including Sly Alley, Steven Sexton, and Logan White-Mulcare.

In addition to Native contributors, we are lucky to have so many dynamic and prolific poets populating urban and rural landscapes up and down the central continental spine. In these pages, you'll find a former U.S. Poet Laureate / Pulitzer Prize winner, Ted Kooser, and numerous state poets laureate: Walter Bargen (Missouri), Benjamin Myers (Oklahoma), David Clewell (Missouri), Nathan Brown (Oklahoma), Dave Parsons (Texas), Jeanetta Calhoun Mish (Oklahoma), Jan Seale (Texas), Carol Hamilton (Oklahoma), and William Trowbridge (Missouri).

The reason for such an anthology at this time is evident. Our lives, thrown into chaos, now eschew once familiar and comfortable artistic / literary logic and justifications. We need a vast national anthology, a recording of before, during, and after moments. As we traverse and live on this terrestrial shell called land / North America / Turtle Island, which provides each of us with food, shelter, water, joy, heartbreak, and so much more, we give you poems about lives, spaces, and places before COVID-19 and before the reckoning of Black Lives Matter.

As it is, we are each connected and disconnected from one another locally and nationally in astounding ways: through both shared and disparate histories, families (and family feuds), pandemics (historic and current), cultural clashes and harmonies / homogeneities and the measured violence of purposeful dislocation and imposed policy of those who create and benefit from such policies and polities. Through it all, I35 poets are writing from spaces familiar to their being / imaginations / stories. The poems and their poets will guide you along a creative corridor overflowing with diverse ecologies, biologies, anthropologies, geographies, hydrologies, ornithologies, and mythologies—rich with testimonies and reflections.

With this, we embark on a poetic journey that traverses along the I35 corridor with similar anxiety and eagerness. As is typical of such an affair, unintended themes emerged, among them: borderland tensions, human relationships (with varying degrees of sexual tension), relationships to place/s, and personal histories with the interstate and with specific places.

Methodology

In the original call for submissions, which we posted in October of 2017, the following mission was articulated:

The I35 Creativity Corridor Poetry Project seeks poetry that embodies many ways of knowing—biology, geology, geography, anthropology, ethnomusicology, and many more—that invoke and evoke creativity as it occurs along or near the major interstate of I35 from Texas (and south to Mexico City) to Minnesota (and north to Ontario).

We seek poems that embody the region/s traversed by I35, Laredo to Duluth, the Rio Grande to Lake Superior, Great Plains to Great Lakes, cotton to wheat to corn to soybeans, from beyond the border to Mexico City / Tenochtitlan (since the roadway runs from Aztec lands to Cree lands in Canada, from Comanche and Kickapoo lands to Pawnee and Osage lands to Ojibwe and Lakota/ Dakota/Nakota lands.

The majority of poets adhered to the mission. Not surprisingly, poets found wonderfully inventive ways to meet it. Some even diverted far afield from the call, which always resulted in long editorial discussions. As you'll see, in a few cases, we included such pieces because they were written upon, within, as a result of being created in proximity to the interstate. In other words, we surmised that a piece could have only been written because of a writer's experience living / being in a specific place—its history, ambiance, and culture. We know place impacts writers. However, creative manifestations occur / emerge out of / because of a constellation of factors. Places create poets as well as poems.

We also sought out and selected an aesthetic array of poets and their poems. Urban poets can be found alongside rural poets. Native and non-Native poets provide varied perspectives regarding land / place. Mexican poets, writing in Spanish, live peacefully among U.S. poets writing in English. Veterans and non-vets equally express devotion to land and freedom of movement. You'll also find three generations of poets (ranging in age from their late 20s to early 80s). Ethnic groups represented include: African American, Anishinaabe, Asian American, Eastern Shawnee, Cherokee, Choctaw, Comanche, Kiowa, Lovelock Paiute, Otoe, Pawnee, and the White Earth Nation.

Note on the Title

The anthology title, *Level Land,* is taken from the 1935 poetry collection of the same name by former University of Oklahoma professor, Kenneth Kaufman (1887-1945), who taught in Modern Languages at the University from 1929 to 1945. He was a creative and instructional force at both at Oklahoma City's Central High School and at OU. The collection's title poem begins:

I think that the mountains shall pass away,
And there shall be no more sea;
But the little hills and the canyons green
And the long level land between
Shall bear forever the prairies sod
And offer their purple flowers to God,
With never a tree to dim the day,
And that is the land for me.

Three stanzas follow in which the speaker recalls visiting other lands: to the sea, mountains ("high hills"), and the forests ("deep woods"), only to reach the final stanza:

So I have come back to the level land,
To a wide, clean land and lone,
Back to the land of the golden plover
And the great white Gulf clouds drifting over.
Oh the smell of corn in the rain at noon!
Oh, the coyote's wail to the winter moon!
Its spell is on me like a brand,
It has marked me for its own.

From *Level Land: A Book of Western Verse*. Dallas, TX: The Kaleideograph Press, 1935. p. 25-26.

We think Kaufman's poem captures an essence of place that aligns with the I35 corridor. Rolling hills / prairies are geographically predominant. So, the book you hold has taken a long journey (Fact: I35 spans just over 1,569 miles in the U.S.), one filled with unanticipated starts and stops, excitement and disappointments, hopes and dashed hopes. We endured because of a singular devotion to the poets whose work we admired. We are grateful to the poets who contributed 140+ poems. Known sarcastically as "fly over" country, we think the poetry demands the I35 corridor be defined as a destination spot featuring the highest levels of creative expression.

Borderlands

No Hay Un Río
Andrea Alzati

no existe un árbol milenario
ninguna colina o cueva
no hay kilómetros de valles
verdes ni nubes barriendo la tierra
una flor desquiciantemente roja en medio de la tierra negra no hay
está solo el cuerpo
huesos aún enteros
por encima del suelo
músculos todavía
blandos y la lengua

no hay un río
no existe limo aquí no
podría arrodillarme en el limo
y mirar lejos y pensar
cualquier cosa porque
aquí no hay lejos
están muy cerca
lás sábanas
de algodón blanco
las camisetas de algodón
de cualquier color
muy cerca y
las líneas que marcan
en el cuerpo

está el cuerpo
blando tibio
huesos todavía
por encima
del suelo

no hay un río
está la palabra río
que no dice agua
no hay una formación de rocas
de más de diez mil años luz
no hay un ave azul cruzando el cielo a las cinco de la tarde

porque aquí no hay cielo
hay espacios vacíos esperando
ser ocupados por una altísima construcción vertical
y el cuerpo
está el cuerpo
sentado lejos
de una pradera limpia cubierta de filas y filas de borregos blancos

There is No River
Translation by Rebecca Zweig

no millennial tree exists
neither hill nor cave
there are no kilometers of green
valleys nor clouds sweeping the earth
an unnaturally red flower in the center of the black earth there is not
it is only the body
bones still whole
above the ground
muscles still
soft and the tongue

there is no river
no silt exists here I could not
kneel in the silt
and look away and think
anything because
here is not far
they're very close
the sheets
of white cotton
the cotton undershirts
of any color
very close and
the lines that mark
in the body

there is the body
soft lukewarm
bones still
above
ground

there is no river
this word river
does not say water
there are not rock formations
more than ten thousand light years
there is not a bluebird crossing the sky at five in the afternoon

because there is no heaven here
there are empty spaces waiting
to be occupied by a towering vertical construction
and the body
there is the body
sitting far away
from a clean meadow covered with rows and rows of white sheep

Movimientos de La Leche
Andrea Alzati

en aquellos días
todas las fuentes
de la ciudad
escupían leche
tan blanca
      que
de haberlas
visto de frente
nos hubieran
dejado ciegos

el humo avanzaba
lentamente
      como
en una procesión religiosa
      y
las preguntas se replicaban
en miles de
formas geométricas
aún sin
nombres

en medio de un silencio
de manteles largos
      y
blanquísimos
frente a una madre
blanquísima
el padre dijo:
—hija, si no fueras mi hija me casaría contigo—

y la hija mostró
el blanco
de sus dientes
en una mueca
      que
bien pudo ser una sonrisa
que opacara lo amargo

como pudo ser su herida
retorciéndose
o de placer
o de un terror
absoluto

con qué soltura puede un perro tirarse a la mitad de la calle.

con qué facilidad
puede una herida
derramar cualquier líquido
transparente
rojo
o de un blanco
tan blanco
que de haberlo
visto de frente
nos hubiera dejado ciegos,
cieguísimos

en aquellos días
toda la calle era
leche blanca
ríos de leche
tan blanca
tan maternal
          que
el instinto materno
también mostraba
su instinto de muerte

—te daré tanta leche que no podrás respirar nunca—

la ciudad era un río de
leche dulce
          que
asfixiaba a cualquiera
          no había dónde esconderse
          no había a dónde correr
la leche entraba
por cualquier orificio

por pequeño que fuera
por debajo de todas las puertas
                    entraban ríos
                              de leche
                                        hirviendo

lo mojaba todo
lo quemaba todo
hasta el esófago
más resistente
tenía úlceras
al rojo
vivo

la hija pensaba
cómo
cómo
cómo
              ¿cómo haré para que
                              las cenizas
                              de mi padre
                                        lleguen a donde
                                        me pidió
                                        claramente
                                        que
                                        tenían que llegar?

          a los once años cualquier petición funeraria es de una solemnidad
inquebrantable.

la ciudad tragaba leche
              como
tragaba cualquier
sustancia líquida
de cualquier herida
que siguiera abierta
por convicción
o por olvido

la ciudad era eso:
una herida hambrienta
buscando a cualquier niña distraída
para arrebatarle
el último aire
        que
le quedara en el pecho,
un pecho
todavía
andrógino

      la ciudad era el lugar perfecto para la asfixia.

la hija buscó piedras
conchas de mar,
dados,
miniaturas de plomo,
vidrios erosionados de colores,
objetos pequeños para levantar
altares diminutos a la materia

una serie
de objetos
chiquititos
donde pudiera
poner sus manos
     sentir con
     los dedos
el peso de
cada objeto
por pequeño
e insignificante
que fuera

la hija guardó semillas rojas
contó del uno al ciento diez
semillas rojas
y las metió en
una botella
de vidrio
verde
      la materia era el lugar perfecto para cifrarse.

la hija guardó cajitas muy pequeñas
adentro de otras cajas
también pequeñas
      y
lo mismo hizo ella:
se guardó en una caja,
en la esquina de una caja
se dedicó devotamente
a dormir

el sueño es
           la única ceremonia
               que
persiste

de día o de noche
dentro o fuera de las sábanas
la hija se dedicó a dormir
      y
a olvidarlo todo
a olvidar su nombre y su apellido
a olvidar si era la hija o el hijo
o si no era nada

(si guardaba silencio
      el tiempo
      suficiente
      en realidad
      no
      era
      nada)

          la ciudad era el lugar perfecto para olvidarlo todo.

en aquellos días
los ríos de leche hirviendo
eran el único alimento posible
no había por qué esperar a
      que
la leche estuviera tibia

también a un líquido hirviendo
el cuerpo
se vuelve invulnerable

el pecho dejó de ser un
pecho andrógino,
la asfixia
        y
el mutismo
en cambio,
serían siempre
andróginos

(las rodillas
las orejas
ciertos ángulos
de las manos...)

                con qué facilidad se puede despreciar la leche materna.

la hija buscó símbolos,
figuras,
trazos,
nombres,
sonidos donde sentarse
a recuperar el habla

la ciudad arrojaba
señales equivocadas
a donde fuera que volteara:
las letras de su nombre
la fecha de tu nacimiento
la fecha del nacimiento de este otro nombre
la dirección de este otro

toda la ciudad
se llenaba de señales
        que
no señalaban nada excepto
        que
la hija había perdido casi toda el habla

la ciudad también era la hija
derramando cualquier cosa
sobre cualquier cuerpo
había
      que
derramarse si quería
conservarse entera

no hay un nombre para cada uno de ellos
todos tenían el mismo nombre:
instinto de vida
instinto de muerte
instinto de ríos de leche

en aquellos días
la ciudad exhalaba
una atmósfera de playa
grotesca, insostenible

la playa
es la muerte del padre
levantándose en olas
      como
un fin
inalterable

              la playa era el lugar perfecto para la indeterminación.

el mar es una muerte
es una espuma
      que
se queda adherida
al cuerpo
      como
un inquilino
      como
un parásito
      como
la palabra muerte
se queda adherida
a las venas

en aquellos días
el mar escupía
peces plateados
el mar era una muerte
era una espuma, una leche
     que
escupía peces
espumas de peces
     que
se adherían al
cuerpo lo
escamaban

       el mar era el lugar perfecto para la muerte.

en aquellos días
la hija se recogía
en su propia compulsión hasta
     que
solamente la compulsión
la movía

en aquellos días
sus manos eran su boca
su boca eran sus manos
todos los movimientos
de la leche sucedían
entre sus manos
     y
su boca

la leche hirviendo
brotaba de su pecho
de todas sus heridas
de todas las fuentes
de la ciudad
en aquellos días
llovía leche hirviendo
sobre la hija
y ella creía
     que

todo eso
era inevitable
la hija
dormía en lo inevitable
se arrodillaba ante lo inevitable
se alimentaba de lo inevitable

los movimientos de la leche
eran inevitables
todos los movimientos
de la herida
de la espuma
de la leche
no había forma de evitarlos

en aquellos días
la hija
era
su propio
alimento

la hija
inflamada
de sí misma
fue arrojada
una vez más
a la intemperie
en aquellos días.

The Movements of Milk
Translation by the author and Marichelo Alzati

in those days
every fountain
in the city
spit milk
so white
     that
if we had seen it
eye to eye
we would have
been blinded

smoke crept
slowly
     as if
in a religious procession
     and
questions
were replicated
in thousands of
geometric shapes
still unnamed

amidst the silence
of long
     and
whitest of tablecloths
facing the
whitest of mothers
the father said:
—daughter, if you weren't my daughter i would marry you—

and the daughter
showed the white of her teeth
in a crooked grin
     that
might have been a smile
to hide the bitterness

as it could have been her wound
writhing
with pleasure
or absolute terror

with such ease can a dog lie in the middle of the street.

with such ease
can a wound
pour any fluid
clear
red
or of a white so white
that if we had seen it
eye to eye
we would have gone
blinder than blind

in those days
the whole street was
white milk
rivers of white milk
so white
so maternal
        that
the maternal instinct
also showed
its death instinct

—i'll feed you so much milk you won't be able to breathe—

the city was a river of milk
so sweet
        that
it could suffocate anyone
        there was no place to hide
        there was no place to run
the milk came in
through any slit
even through the tiniest slit
beneath every door

                boiling milk
                        rivers

                                came in

it soaked everything
it burnt everything
even the most
resistant esophagus
had red-hot
ulcers

the daughter thought
how
how
how
            how will i
            get my father's ashes
            to the place where

                                he clearly told me
                                they had
                                to be?

        at age eleven any funerary request holds an unbreakable solemnity.

the city swallowed milk
        as it
swallowed any
fluid from any
wound that
was still open
by conviction
or forgetfulness

the city was that:
a hungry wound
searching for any distracted girl
to take from her
any last breath
        that
she still held in her chest
a chest

still
androgynous

       the city was the perfect place for suffocation.

the daughter searched for stones
seashells,
a pair of dice,
lead miniatures,
colorful sea glass,
small objects with which
she could raise
tiny altars to matter

a series of
tiny objects
where she could
lay her hands on
      and feel with
      her fingers
the weight of
every object
no matter
how little
and how insignificant
it may be

the daughter collected red seeds
counting from one to one hundred and ten
red seeds
she put them
inside a
green
glass
bottle

      matter was the perfect place to disclose.

the daughter collected
really tiny boxes
that she put inside

other boxes
          and
she did the same:
she gathered herself
inside a box
in the corner of a box
and devoted herself
to sleep

sleep is
          the only ceremony
          that
persists

at daytime or nighttime
inside or outside the sheets
the daughter devoted herself to sleep
          and
forget everything
forget her name and last name
forget if she was the daughter or the son
or if she was nothing

(if she kept silent
          long enough
          she really
          was nothing)

          the city was the perfect place for oblivion.

in those days
rivers of boiling milk
were the only nourishment possible
there was no need to wait
          for
the milk to be tepid

to a boiling fluid
the body
also becomes invulnerable

the chest was no longer
an androgynous chest,
suffocation
           and
silence
on the other hand
would always be
androgynous

(the knees
the ears
some angles
of the hands...)

           with such ease one can despise maternal milk.

the daughter searched for symbols,
figures,
strokes,
names,
sounds
where she could sit
and recover speech

the city uttered
the wrong signs
anywhere she looked at:
the letters of his name
your date of birth
some other name's date of birth
some other's address

all the city
filled up with signs
           that
indicated nothing except
           that
the daughter had almost lost all form of speech

the city was also the daughter
pouring anything

on any
body
     she
had to pour
if she wanted
to remain complete

there is no name for each one
they all had the same name:
life instinct
death instinct
milk river instinct

in those days
the city exhaled
a grotesque, unsustainable
beach atmosphere

the beach
is the father's death
rising in waves
     as
an immutable
end

        the beach was the perfect place for indetermination.

the sea is a death
a spume
     that
sticks to
the body
     as a
tenant
     as a
parasite
     as
the word death
sticks to the veins

in those days
the sea spit
silvery fish
the sea was a death
was a spume, was a milk
      that
spit fish
spumes of fish
      that
sticked to
the body
they scaled it

      the sea was the perfect place for death.

in those days
the daughter gathered
in her own compulsion until only
compulsion itself
moved her

in those days
her hands were her mouth
her mouth was her hands
all the movements of the milk
happened
between her mouth
      and
her hands

the boiling milk
welled up from her chest
from all her wounds
from all the fountains
in the city

in those days
boiling milk rained
over the daughter
and she thought

        that
all this
was inevitable
the daughter
slept in the inevitable
kneeled before the inevitable
fed from the inevitable

the movements of the milk
were inevitable
all the movements
of the wound
of the spume
of the milk
there was no way to avoid them

in those days
the daughter
was her own
nourishment

the daughter
swollen
with herself
was tossed
once more
to inclemency
in those days.

Field Guide Ending in a Deportation
Marcelo Hernandez Castillo

I confess to you my inadequacies. I want to tell you things I do not know about myself. I've made promises to people whom I will never see again. I've cried in an airport bathroom stall in El Paso, TX when immigration denied my father's application. It felt like a mathematical equation—everything on one side needed to equal everything on the other. It almost made sense to be that sad. I am not compelled to complicate this metaphor. I'm selling this for two dollars. Years ago, on my birthday, I came out to my friends. I thought about the possibility of painting their portraits. What a stupid idea. I've started to cover up certain words with Barbie stickers in my journal. It occurs to me, sitting in my car at a Dollar General parking lot in search of cheap balloons for a party which I do not care about, that I am allowed my own joy. I pick the brightest balloons, pay, drive home, and dress for the party. I mouth the words happy birthday to you in a dark room lit by everyone's phone cameras. Afterwards, I enter all of my emails from five years into a cloud engine and the most used word is ok. I confess that I have had a good life. I spend many nights obsessing over the placement of my furniture. I give you my boredom. I give you my obligation. I give you the night I danced and danced and danced at a child's birthday party, drunk and by myself. I've been someone else's shame. It's true, at its core, amá was deported because she was hit by a car. For years to come, this will be the ending of a sad joke she likes to tell. I laugh each time she tells the joke to strangers. Something about how there is more metal than bone in her arm. Something about a magnet. She says I thought I had died and death meant repeating a name forever. She says el jardin encierra la boca de mis pasos. But this is a bad translation. It's more like I felt like a star, I felt like somebody famous.

Immigration Interview with Don Francisco
Marcelo Hernandez Castillo

In the church was the deepest
well of the city where the priest
was lowered every morning.
[*Please say more*]
I've split open the small fish
and counted the candles tucked inside—
all the pink nails tapping the wicks.
[*Please elaborate*]
If I had children,
there would be no reason
to empty the bowls
stagnant with rain water—
no reason at all to keep saying
"you are almost."
[*Please say more*]
The wasps: their multitude of clapping hands.
[*Please elaborate*]
How small the dolls.
How insignificant
the hands that move them.
[*Please say more*]
Perhaps the butterflies are mute because
no one would believe their terrible stories.

Immigration Interview with Jay Leno

Marcelo Hernandez Castillo

What is your objective?
To return all the children
hidden behind the street lamps.
How long do you plan on staying here?
I don't understand
the question.
I said, how long do you plan on staying here?
We would have drowned
even without our laughter.
Is that really your name?
Yes, the clothes on the floor
blossomed like the orchards in spring.
Have you been here before?
There was a man who knew the way.
I put his fingers in my mouth
when he pointed in the direction of the sun.
Who are you wearing?
The woman gave birth in the dark.
I thought I felt hands where there were none.
Everyone dug a useless hole.
Are you alone?
North was whichever way
the mannequins were pointing.
The softest bone was the one
that burned the longest.
Do you cry at night?
Are you alone right now?

Wetback

Marcelo Hernandez Castillo

After the first boy called me a wetback,
I opened his mouth and fed him a spoonful of honey.
I like the way you say "honey," he said.
I made him a necklace out of the bees that have died in my yard.
How good it must have felt before the small village
echoed its grief in his throat, before the sirens began ringing.
How fallow their scripture.
Perhaps we were on stage which meant it was a show,
which meant our only definition of a flower was also a flower.
I waved to the crowd
like they taught me,
like a mini-miss something.
Thank you.
Thank you.
Yes, I could have ripped open his throat.
I could have blown him a kiss from the curtain.
I wanted to dance by myself in a dark room
filled with the wingless bodies of bees—
to make of this our own Old Testament
with all the same beheaded kings
pointing at all the same beheaded prophets.
The same Christ running through every door
like a man who forgot his child in the car.
But the lights were too bright.
I couldn't hear him because I wasn't on stage.
I could have been anyone's
idea of pity.
How quiet our prophets.
Let my bare back remind him of every river he's swam in.
Miel and *miel*.
I pulled the bees off the string
and cupped them in my palm.
I told him my Spanish name.
There was nothing dry on my body—
The lamps falling over in the dark of me.

Hands Off, Rivera
Chuck Etheridge

For Diana

Diego Rivera had a time machine.
He put a picture of you on a wall in Mexico City,
Painting your Puebla beauty,
Capturing your thick, brown hair,
Your heart-shaped face,
Your full lips,
Your strong brown arms,
Held in a feminine curve,
Your narrow waist
And sexy broad hips
Rendered in enough sensual detail
That I want to find him and punch him in the face.
How dare he tag a government building
With a sexy picture
Of my wife?

I don't care
That he died
Before you were born,
Or that this picture
Is great art.
That's my wife, Diego.
Keep your philandering eyes
Off of her.
God knows
You had enough women—
Leave Diana alone.

But as she and I age,
As the hair greys,
Sight worsens,
The hips and arms get arthritic,
I get a little more forgiving
Of Mr. Rivera,
And I am glad you are there,
On a wall,
Looking as fresh

As the day I met you.
Assuming the Mexican government
Cooperates,
Does what is called 'historic preservation,'
You'll be there on that wall
For all of our anniversaries to come,
There for our children's children to see,
In your young, beautiful Glory.

So if I find him,
Maybe I'll just chastise Diego for his wandering eye,
And then I'll say,
"She's nice to look at,
Isn't she?"

And he'll say,
"You're a lucky man.
I looked at her and painted her,
But you got to live a life with her."

Crossing the Border at Laredo
Carol Hamilton

3rd busiest port in the U.S., they told us.
"I wouldn't take them there
now," he said, of the young people,
we in his church basement
overnight en route to Monterrey
for work in a boys' school.
"I was scared when I saw you
arguing with the border guards
with their machine guns,"
one man told me. Not everyone
brought an original copy
of their birth certificate.

Another trip the inspectors
demanded money for the bribe
be slipped across the leather
beneath the steering wheel
to avoid security cameras.

As the officials began unloading
the trailer, she crossed
with her new husband
to El Norte, his homeland.
They almost immediately
came upon the photo of her,
hands together, eyes heavenward,
she in white for confirmation.
The search immediately ceased,
the trailer re-loaded and
the newlyweds waved on through.

Our midnight crossing on a Mexican bus
from Chicago to Guanajuato,
the passport in my purse,
the (how could I?!) out-of-date one,
my terror before the border official
palpable ... but he smiled,
waved me on, no fee,

though our bus driver sent us back
a second time, saying there were
no exceptions. That night
there were exceptions.
The grim U.S. officials on our return
ignored our U. S. passports
as they checked and re-checked
all the Mexican ones.

All the way here to anywhere
on I35, a journey
of constant construction zones
shrouded in fumes from impatient cars
waiting, waiting, the air heavy.
The cars and cars
and the trucks, the trucks,
the trucks, everything passes
through Laredo, except
for one thing—understanding.

Fireworks
Kevin Prufer

He believed that great literature was elastic,
and by this he meant that it shaped itself to the concerns
of each new generation of readers. Homer,
he often said, is *elastic*. We cannot read him
as Greeks, so we read him as ourselves
and find in him exactly what we are looking for.
Shakespeare. Elastic. Milton. Et cetera.

+

You're going to do it,
                              you said, and I said,
Of course I'm going to do it, and I struck the match
and for a moment
                         your face glowed yellow in its light,
and then I lit the fuse—

+

His mother had died. And later, his father had died,
painfully. So now he had no one, or so he thought.
And it was a comfort that books might speak to him
in ways that were intimate and new, that this
was part of their fundamental design,
                                        the dead
speaking to the living.

+

—and up to the heavens with the rocket
while you caught your breath
                              and the black sky ripped
with color, one rocket after another, and *Oh*, you said,
as I lit each fuse.
                    Hard to believe
the whole field would catch,
                                 though it was the dry season,
late July, and the tall grasses took the flame

50

easily,
        and mostly I remember running from there—

+

God or his parents whispering to him through
the pages of books.
                They spoke to him on rainless days,
his father cleaning his boots, the smell of black polish,
the sound of the brush,
                his mother turning the page—

+

Don't move, I said, as we watched the field burn
from behind the trees—waves of black smoke
that obliterated the barns behind them,

the circle of flame
widening. Thus the field opened
                  like an eye

+

and the young man looked up from his book.
He had read it before,
                Achilles in the land of the dead,
mists rising off the water, the smoking dead—

What did it mean?
          His mind
had drifted.
        His father brushing his boots until, *Darling*,
his mother said, *must you do that at the table?*
And, *Yes*, his father said, holding up the polished boot,
                           I must.

+

It meant the following:
The wind was strong.
          The fire devoured the field,

then it jumped to the brush by the barn,
then to the barn itself,
which caught quickly.

A single horse cowered among the hay bales,
its oily hair glowing bluely
                              as the flames approached it—

+

Calm down, you said.
                    No one will know
a thing.
            We have to get out of here
is all, and then we were running toward the car.

+

By god, I'd rather slave on earth for another man—
some dirt-poor tenant farmer who scrapes to keep alive—
than rule down here over all the breathless dead,
                                        said Achilles
from the burning fields.
                        His father caught beneath the tractor's tire
gasped once more, then relaxed
                        in the field.
And now the young man was alone,
                            looking over the field
that in another part of this poem
                        I burned with my friend.

And who could account for such desolation,

reading a book by the window,
parentless and alone,
                    dry fields, perturbed by wind and sunlight—

+

And then the horse burst through the barn doors
and galloped into the field next door,

                                    its flaming body
glowing orange and blue in the night,
                                    and it set that field afire,
too,
    before it stumbled once, twice, and fell, smoking, onto its side—

+

and in this way, the young man thought,
laying down his book,
while his father put his boots away
and his mother sighed,
                    and in this way,
literature is handed on from one generation
to the next.

The Translator
Kevin Prufer

A poem in translation,
                                    the young man was fond of saying,
is like the dead body of a foreigner
                                    washed up on our shores.
                                                            Here
he usually paused to let the metaphor sink in.

Some members of the audience nodded thoughtfully.

I will now read from my translations of a little-known ancient Roman poet,
he told them,
            shuffling his papers, then looking into

                                            the dark
half-empty auditorium.

+

The dead body refused to be still.   The waves
loved it too much,
                pushing it onto the beach, then rolling it
seaward again.
                And so it made its way down the beach,
alighting for a moment
                        or several moments,
                                        on the wet sand,
then bobbing out
            among the American swimmers.

+

120 foreigners in a leaking boat
is too many,
            so the ocean fills with poems. Some retain
the qualities of their original language,
                                but others sink blackly
into a new language.

+

             Here I am, out here! I can see your
oil rigs glittering on the horizon,
                  says the young woman whom no one
listens to. Or,
        she says nothing,
clinging to the side of the waterlogged boat,
where she has floated all night
              among the drifting bodies.

A few of them became tangled among the oil rigs,
while others arrived
          gently on our shore.

+

A poem that has floated some distance
from its accident
         transforms—so the people
ran away in horror
          when at last he came to rest
on a crowded part of the beach.

+

You foreigners in your many-sailed ships,
come join the empire! the translator intones
           from his spot-lit podium,
and the audience sighs.
        Here I am, out here,
says a little voice in the translation,
          a voice no one,
not even the translator,
      can hear.

+

The audience
had come to hear a lecture on poetry in translation

and now the translator was going on
about the ancient Roman tendency to absorb,
and therefore transform,
                        foreign cultures,
their gods and foods.

Outside the auditorium, it had grown dark,
a perfect summer night.
                        The thousand vessels
on the great black ocean
glittered and loomed

+

                        and for days, bodies
washed up on the beach.
                        Now, the American workers
zippered them into vinyl bags,

which, in the translator's metaphor,
constitutes a kind of publication.

+

 But what is there to say
                        about that young woman
still clinging to the wreckage
two days into my poem?
                        A gentle summer rain
prickles her skin. *Here I am,* she says,
looking toward the oil rigs hunkering between her
and the shore.
                Here I am.

+

She is a very fine woman
and someone should translate her.

Hog Kaput

Kevin Prufer

Because we couldn't control their population
and because they destroyed our parks
and farmlands,
        we proposed
to place in troughs a kind of poison
called Hog Kaput.
        The poison, a blood thinner, killed
humanely,
        and in the video we presented to the legislature,
the hog in the lab took only a few steps
before falling on its side.

\+

        Hello,
said the feeding trough to the hungry hog.
Come here.
        At first, the hog eyed the metal trough
with suspicion. He'd grown accustomed
to the pleasures of the farmer's field
        and that place
by the riverbank where the wild blackberry brambles
tickled his hide.
        How the sunlight dappled
the muddy water and warmed his thick neck. *C'mon,*
said the trough, and the hog
        lumbered over,
lifted the lid with his snout, sniffed the pellets,
pushed his face inside.

\+

        Heavy as shit, said the workman
after he'd removed the dead hog from the testing room,
hosed the floor clean,
        and washed his hands.
Heavy as shit, he told the pregnant young woman
he'd married one year before, exactly,

who sat across from him
while the waiter set two bowls of soup gracefully
on the table,
            gotta feel bad for the poor fucker,
he said,
        and she smiled because, yes, his wasn't an easy job,
but somebody, she told herself, somebody
                                had to do it.

+

By any definition,
                    they were an invasive species,
and the citizen farmers asked only
that their lands not be disturbed.
                            Shooting them
from helicopters
                accomplished little—there were just
too many—
                and even if we unintentionally
poisoned scavengers that fed on their meat,
it was a small price to pay
to keep our American parks
                            untrammeled,
and to satisfy our farmers—

+

You see,
he told his pregnant wife,
                    the trouble is they reproduce, so two of
them
become a thousand,
                    and pretty soon it's hogs everywhere,
hogs like you wouldn't believe,
                        roving gangs of hogs,
and she blew gently on the spoonful of soup,
sipped it,
        then looked up, smiling.

+

It tasted of carrot, it tasted
of wild potato, burdock root and turnip, parsnip
and sunchoke,
                    and the hog ate and ate from the trough,
until he had his fill.
                    Then the lid snapped shut,
and he took a step toward the river,
                              where the others
lay on the banks in sunlight,
                          and from the corners of his eyes,
a delightful sparkling,
                      a kind of flicker, a thousand
fireflies crowding his vision,
                          beautiful, really,
and he took another step
                              into what was now
a kind of snowstorm—

+

                    So we can have meat for the table,
so we can protect the fields,
                          because some species are
invasive,
          because our country needs protection,
because we inhabit the land
the way an ideal
                  inhabits the mind—
we submitted our proposal to the legislature,
hoping they would understand why it was vital that,
at all costs,
          we saw to the elimination of the hogs.

+

Yes, he said, it had been a very good meal,
a nice anniversary,
                    his wife was happy, yes, she was,
he could tell because,
                    when he helped her into the car,
then leaned inside to hand her the Styrofoam box

filled with leftovers,
                she reached out to him,
surprised him,
             kissing him suddenly on the mouth,
and squeezing his hand.
                So now, driving home
past the fields, now empty of hogs,
with her beside him—
              the three of them, really,
if you counted the baby—
             well, who could be happier
than he was?

Margaritas and Redfish
Ken Hada

I.

She should have had more sense
than to fall in love with a fisherman

She knows he knows hooks
knows how to hold slippery fish
knows quiet dark hours
the web of net, the touch of line

Waters always move
but she would not flow with them

He reads sunrise on a morning stream
sunset on the Delta Coast

It's all one—this he knows
this she tries to forget

II.

Some nights I just feel like driving
and never stopping
Interstate 35 rarely opens like the Red Sea
Moses must have known something strange was up
What happened to the fish, Moses?

Austin radio will take me to Waco
At Waco I'll find some station until Fort Worth
to Oklahoma City—tonight
I may wind up in Canada

Driving under a rustler's moon
the friendly dark accepts my searching mood
echoes my empty words
It's not bitterness
It's just that some things don't make sense

Cheer up, things could be worse
Sure enough, I cheered up
and things got worse
This night driving
is like night fishing—you wonder
how your lines will return

III.

Margaritas and Redfish make fine dining
A band plays in the next room—
CCR, Stones, ZZ Top, Orbison—
all the standards

Raise a glass to the music
smile at the pretty lady
notice her eyes dancing
as she sings along

Taste blackened redfish
wild rice and white wine
think of a fisherman
how life would be without him
how some lonely leathered man on the Gulf
tends his morning nets
much the same as you

      beneath a twinning sun
          –a twinning sun

Cool Tiles
Gene Novogrodsky

No, I didn't know Miriam Rodriguez,
Killed in San Fernando, Tamaulipas, Mexico,
For trying to find those disappeared daily...
Usually teens, their mothers wondering, waiting...
Rodriguez, just another government-recorded number in Mexico's
thousands dead in a decade
of blood

***

I moved quickly past Rodriguez, how easy from safety...
San Fernando for me, a San Fernando close in years:
Sorghum deep red.
Beans so green.
Fields so flat, with low down hills and the Gulf east,
High hills and blue mountains west.
Slow streams, a slow river.
Green tractors, green combines, black pickups.
Cool stucco homes.
Buses pulsing in the cool station.
Fumes sour sweet.
Bakery screen doors banging,
Empanandas and rolls warm.
Restaurants, plates and drinks...
Fruit carts, melons, pineapple...
Hardware stores, nails, wire...
Taco wagons, smoke off coals...
Corn wagons, steam rises...
Tires, gasoline...
Then, to the narrow, iron bridge to the south,
Green brush on sluggish riverbanks.
Or, then to the flat to the north...
Dusty fields stretch...
Goats nibbling bark,
Horses stretch into watering tubs,
Cattle finds stubble.

***

Miriam Rodriguez, am I trite at your end?
And since I did not know you,
I rest on the tiles, touch them,
Homes, large and small,
Tree-circled or bare,
Garages and canvas,
Tiled patios,
Cool tiles,
Swept and washed daily,
Red tiles...
A summer sun hot,
Crops, trees, flowers droop,
And those tiles, so cool...
Perhaps you fell to such when shot, bleeding...
Your warm blood to the square-set red tiles...
And there you rest,
In your San Fernando,
Even my San Fernando...

***

Dare I claim its hold from but two fast hours afar?
And, a teen taken,
A reporter killed,
A soldier wounded,
A store boarded,
A barn burned,
Family packed, gone in night's dark...
Miriam Rodriguez, no flight for her...

281

Gene Novogrodsky

281, from South Texas to the Canadian border.

The migrant highway.

Listen to the songs,

Always accordions.
Read the short stories,

Loss, movement, broken trucks.

Take some early July time past

Dry sorghum and corn stalks,
Yellow brown, harvested.
Heavy green sugar cane, river watered...
The mid-summer usual,

Not the findings:
A red and white Santa Claus cap,
Coiled tape measures,
Dead dried sharp-toothed possums,

Fur baked on asphalt.

Dead dried sharp-toothed armadillos,

Gray shells cracked on asphalt.

Shacks with hung clothes drifting in 100-degree heat,

Cars rusting on blocks.

Gated homes, automatic garage door openers,

Circular pools, tepid blue water.

Who tossed the Santa Claus cap?

Traveling North: The Rules
Jan Seale

Mile 49: Ladies and gentlemen,
UnitedStatesImmigrationCheckpoint coming
up! Please have your documentation ready.
¡Damas y caballeros tambien!

Now there must be a neatening—
all things vertical, horizontal, squared:
hats removed, hair smoothed, hats replaced;
pant legs worked back down the thighs;
boot toes polished on backs of opposing calves;
lipstick checked; long hair slung-brushed;
babies taken off breast; blouses closed;
waking of older children, Sit up!

Now the *papeles*, always the *papeles*:
from shirt pockets, billfolds, purses,
bosoms, boot tops, jean pockets.
You unfold your *papeles*
or take your card from its holder:
Do you look like your picture?
Hold your life steady;
practice holding your future
steady in your hands.

The driver will pull into the port.
Stop talking. Cross yourself.
Immigration Checkpoint! He will climb down.
Look clean; look bright;
look like your picture ID.

La Migra will board.
(*La Migra* is not kidding.)
Have your *papeles* ready.
¡Buenas tardes! He will speak
kind to the *viejos* on the front seat.

La Migra starts down the aisle.
You citizens?

You?
This your bag?
La Migra looks at each passenger,
takes the *papeles*, studies them,
pats the seatback as he passes.

La Migra checks the bathroom.
(You better not be in it.)
Now he returns, his boots sounding.
He will be looking for telltale signs.
(You better not be handing your *papeles*
back to your friend just yet.)

It is almost over. Everyone is fine...
—wait! He's asking that gringo hippie,
What you doing down in the Valley?

Nothing, man!
That *bolillo*! He doesn't know the rules!
For that he goes with *La Migra*,
keeps us all here, waiting.

Would he empty, please,
the contents of his purple nylon bag
onto the table? Another guy comes.
They take up a book and shake it
like something might fall out.
They examine another object.
Someone looking safely out the window:
Eh, *estúpidos*! That's a *capo* for a guitar,
not a roach clip! The bus laughs.

The gringo hippie is allowed back.

When the bus is under way again,
food will break out all over:
empanadas, gorditas, fruta,
Cocas, Topo Chico.

¡Gracias a Dios! a *viejita*
will breathe it.
An old cowboy will hear.
¡Palabra! No kidding!

Sailing Over the Moon on I-35
Jan Seale

For Charles

How you called from Dallas to see if
I was still coming to the state fair,
how I said I'd lost the will, then you told me
about your tests for vertigo, and at the end
of possible diagnoses we wondered silently
if this was not the beginning of ailments
that would finally halt the merriment of friendship;

How I suddenly remembered the total lunar eclipse
beginning at 9:11 (why, oh why that time?)
and, not wanting our connection broken,
how we hurried out to our respective yards,
phones pressed to our heads,
you between fir and elm,
I between palm and mesquite
and began to co-narrate the celestial event;

How it was a luminous fingernail at first,
yet I observed the other side faintly glowing.
(You could not see the other side prompting you
to say you had not had your glasses changed
in several years. Well, then no wonder, I said,
but it's just a fingernail, though I willed you
to see the umbra and after a while, you did);

How the fingernail was being trimmed by the earth,
bursting in with the astronomy scissors,
while we asked each other, Is it smaller where you are?
Laughing, as if we could know...
then Nah, the distance between us is nothing at all
compared to what the earth is from the moon tonight,
hugging as it is, the short side of its ellipsis;

And though we didn't make Guinness,
I awoke next morning to think of the numbers:
60 years between us since high school,

500 miles the interstate between us,
220,000 miles the moon's wink,
we in a giant triangulation with it
from our respective driveways,
aware of your vertigo, my bad ear,
your heart valve, my heartache,
thinking this might be our only time
to share a celestial event;

But how maybe next year we could try
to close in on the state fair and ride
the round moon of the ferris wheel together.

Ocotillo

C.R. Resetarits

Desert meadow
ballerinas
in fifth position

moon caught
monsoon released
full corps staging

sway, turn
pricked pirouette
flame blooms tipping

fingers in this
land of odd quivers
and skyward arms.

Or ancient occupants
of open, stony
of desert slopes.

Bajada
ocotillo
are firebirds, are

lunar troops
arms raised
to heaven

are archers,
flame fingered
earth arcing

are weird warriors,
curious creatures stirred
by summer's sky-slit rains.

Inner Space
Shin Yu Pai

a guide aims her flashlight
at the borehole drilled
half a century before

the build of I-35, below
ground it's twenty degrees
cooler than the blazing temps

out there, the cavern where
my Texan mate takes me to find
relief from heat, beneath a canopy

of pencil-thin soda straw
stalactites, the Permian
floodwater maze that claimed

the lives of Ice Age species, mammoth

armadillo and sabre-toothed cat,
swamped in quicksand, a pyramid
of bat guano piled high

on the grotto floor,
grows taller with time,
past the talus cone of

bone sink I spot a crumbling
tusk, tongue my upper molar
claimed by dental caries

capped one month ago
in gold, what relics
what remains hereafter

Calpurnia in Tejas

Desiree Morales

Two thousand children
in the tented desert.
By then you're past
tense. Hysterical
 is a word that sometimes
gets used here.

Listen, I read about minority stress
and frankly they should call
them micro-murders.

I tell my heart to behave.

Amygdala sharpens a knife.

Listen, there are already
mass graves in Tejas, unearthed
years before this panic. By the time
it's the truth, the truth
is already ashes in your mouth.

I tell my heart—but you can't force
the heart.

Amygdala on a short leash.

How long before—Listen.
What you fear will happen has
already happened. I didn't
want to be right, but
here we are

Turkey Pastoral
Scott Weaver

They are waiting when we return
and manage to somehow both strut and wobble
about the backyard where the cedar
post barbwire fence marks off
our small plot of world.

It's the fact of their feathered bodies,
so unlike their plastic-wrapped avatars
I soak in olive oil and thyme,
shove into the oven, worry eight hours over
that sets me stalking them
in sneakers and jeans, caffeine,
nicotine and late-afternoon bourbon
joyriding my bloodstream
like a pack of teenagers roaming suburban savannahs
sniffing the air for the scent of new death.

The turkey last in line looks up at me
as if I've just appeared in its office doorway
with another dumb request.
I see them each so clearly.
I feel ever-present and without end.
I can touch them, I think, if I stay
low and slow and blend my body's
awkward lines into the cactus-dotted
yellow rock behind me.

So I am surprised that they shuffle out of the yard
because who knew turkeys move with such dignity,
and once they're through the generous gap in the fence
each is lost to me into what passes now for the wild.

Three turkeys quick and fat with unconcern,
they forget me here hunched, eyes gleaming,
full of that sort of religious feeling
people like us catch when we forget ourselves
to ignore the rest of the world when we're dreaming
that we are the last, best thing.

Five o'Clock Traffic
Lisa L. Moore

At first my eyes slide past the begging bowl,
above the grimy hands, cans and old clothes,
to meet fierce eyes above a dirty beard.
Drive on. Rear view: I glimpse a sudden flutter,
an arm extends to perch a flash goldfinch
I didn't know was there. Things happen

with and without us. The goldfinch happens,
glimpse of roadside grace, a strike that bowls
me over with my undeserving. Goldfinch,
rising from the ashes of old clothes.
Jerking eyes to road, I feel a flutter
of fear, slam brakes, avoid an over-beered

driver. Hasn't seen the light, his beard
a whisker past the hour of five. It happens
quickly: vision, threat of death, the flutter
of gold no one knows you saw, a tree bole
t-boned in the driver's side, today's clothes
suddenly on-site ID. Goldfinch,

you almost got me. Not today, Goldfinch.
Itching past my grasp, brittle joy beards
the lion, my head in its jaws. Near-death clothes
me in grateful sweat. It could have happened.
Terror is its own cure, smoking bowl
undrinkable till cooled by exhale's flutter.

I turn at the light. Unknown flags flutter
above the Stop-n-Shop marquee, goldfinch-
yellow, raven-black, jay-green, the bowl
of evening sky purpling behind the beard
of the Blue Genie mascot. Who happens
to step out but you! I know your clothes.

Under the choked highway, thick dust clothes
the low angle of the sun. I flutter
fingers, greet and say goodbye. It happens

as lights change. A violet sky fits
inside my windshield, a sage's dirty beard
has made this place more holy. I fill his bowl.

In my old clothes, I'm no golden goldfinch
but I'm flattered to be asked for bread,
to tender, perhaps, an internal bow.

Plato's Right
Lisa L. Moore

Yesterday I came back home again—
another work trip. Gold, you kept the home
fires burning. Yearning? There was some
while I was gone, but it's the end
of Sunday dinner, full with cousins come
to visit, so we just exchange a thumbs-
up, sweet kiss, warm hug. You used to bend
me backwards over couches in your ardor.
With kids and in-laws, aches and pains, it's harder
to dance that dance. I miss it, but I'm glad
we had it, jeweled years alone and mad
about each other's bodies. Plato's right.
Lust leads us on. Remember, gem, that night,
our first, you asked me why we're here?
I answered: divine love. That's also why we're queer.

San Antonio
W. Jackson Rushing III

When we come down the old oxen road
wild mustang grapes vined around the fence posts,
the dank ammonia of polecat perfume heavy in the air.
Johnny Texas, I recall, burned his hand and his momma did too
picking such fruit. The wagon wheels sank into deep ruts,
cavernous army-issue trunks groaned as they rose abruptly
and fell against the coarse ribs, and gov't mules shone with
sweat. In my pocket I had a picture postcard, folded and
creased, stolen from my auntie's album, which showed Satank
and other Kiowa chiefs gathered under cottonwood.
I spoke a little English at least, but not my kin
and we camped near to some other Germans along the Guadalupe.
My grandpa's discharge papers said "wounded by a spent shot"
and his boots didn't hardly fit anymore. We saw a sign
for bad water, drunken soldiers roasting dog meat by a treaty oak,
and a crescent moon over a grove of pecan trees
when we come down the old oxen road.

The Geography of Need
Sandra Soli

A Choral Performance Poem for Several Voices, dedicated to
the victims of human smuggler James Matthew Bradley, one
of many operating in the I-35 corridor. Judge speaks prose.

[Music]   Samuel Barber's *Adagio for Strings*,
               establish theme 8 seconds, then down an under
               opening voice. Music Out as gavel strikes.

Judge/Announcer] James Matthew Bradley, you have pleaded
               innocent to conspiracy to transport and harbor im
               migrants for financial gain resulting in death. Ten
               deaths, Mr. Bradley, following your arrest at the I-35
               North on-ramp in San Antonio, Texas. Human traf
               ficking, murder of ten, attempted murder and tor
               ture of 180-plus men and four juveniles packed into
               your truck as cargo.

[Sound]   Courtroom gavel strikes twice.

[Judge/Announcer] What have you to say?

[Bradley]   I didn't know there was people, Judge.
               I hired on to drive that rig to Kansas.
               Met a guy at WalMart for keys.

[Men's Voices] A matter of la economía.
               We paid their price.
               We were promised America.

[One man]   I had job cutting wheat.

[Young Voice] Mi abuelo paid bribe.
               Five thousand dollars. (Sob) Abuelito!

[Men, in tandem] You took a piss. We hollered. You have ears.

               Give us water. Give us light. (fading) wa ____ ter.

[Bradley]   Yes, Sir. Some banging. Ropes, chain,
               stuff not tied down. At fill-up, got to talkin' to cashier,
               drank a soda.

[Men's Voices]	Del Norte dreams. Then daynight. Darkness. We were cattle.
[Bradley]	Meant to check that rattle.
[One Boy]	Papi no más. No más.
[Bradley]	Almost two hundred? No way! Ten dead? What?
[Men]	Policía opened doors. Some of us ran. Stopped in parking lot. Dropped in grass. Too weak.
[One man]	San Antonio to Laredo, 101 outside. For us, worse. Dropped our clothes. No air, no water.
[Men]	No air, no light. A locked truck. You knew. You knew all the time.
[Bradley]	Guy I replaced said truck was empty, Judge. Sure I heard noise. Wind howls on the highway.
[Men]	No air, no water. Sick.
[Bradley]	I needed money. Quick cash.
[One Voice]	No light. Then light. The sun that killed us revealed our glistening bodies.
[Boys]	What you planned in darkness took us to heaven.
[Bradley]	Swear to Jesus, Judge. I did not know. Did not . . . know.
[Sound]	Gavel strikes once.
[Judge/Announcer]	Postscript. In October, 2017 James Matthew Bradley changed his plea to guilty. Prosecutors did not seek the death penalty. On April 20, 2018, Bradley was sentenced to life in prison.

Texas Road Trip
Catherine A. Lee

My mother comes from snowy Massachusetts,
savors February heat and redbuds blooming
Texas Mountain Laurel bursting its near grapey scent.

Craving BBQ, GPS directs our Lockhart
road trip to a blessed lot where
many cop cars park for lunch.

We northeast tourists marvel when a wizened
woman gathers butcher paper into handy basins
for buying brisket by the piled-on pound.
No plates, no sauce, plastic utensils
may be requested by the dainty.

Then heading off to Smitty's in a smaller
once-was-Kreuz location. On "smoking" side,
the room recalls our Jersey grandma's
basement coal-stoked furnace,
but this is a Texas oakwood-fired pit.

Yet more brisket beckons but
we're stuffed and driving home
the scenic route through
what locals call Hill Country.
My oily oozing palms are
sticking to a tacky steering wheel.
Near Canyon Lake, mom says
she's feeling clog of arteries,
heartbeat slowing to a crawl.
Passing site of dead deer fallen
by the side of highway,
vultures feasting on its carcass,
my omnivorous mother says,
"I'm ready to be veggie now."

Color of Mourning

Dave Parsons

She awakened to Texas summer bright
in her eyes; throwing on a new yellow
robe, she dragged her body into the kitchen
to make coffee which she dug from a deep
yellow decanter. Awareness steeps through
the heart beating perks, her eyes fall on the child's
drawing that was stuck on the refrigerator door,
a yellow duck swimming on deep dark
water under another bloody sun brimming
with amber iris—Iris, goddess of the rainbow,
adding to the litany of golden messengers, all
bringing to her mind the dress, the yellow
dress that she had given to her niece
for her fifth birthday, the sweet lemon
yellow dress that the child delighted in so
that today she was to be buried in it—the sanctuary
of the summer kitchen felt unusually cold
as she cracked a single egg, spilling
carefully the delicate yoke onto melting butter
thinking, yellow—yellow—
yellow should not feel like this.

Ghost Hawk
Dave Parsons

After William Wenthe's, Desconsado

I too remember driving the predawn highways
leaving Amarillo south toward the ebbing
darkness before the blooming pregnant glowing
morning, comfy within the moving blind
of creature comforts; temp controls, corduroy jeans,
Starbucks aroma filling all—all those interior voids
without the yap, yap, yapping of morning radio,
opting for the birthing silence of Texas prairie,

the ghost like shadows flashing by, glimpsed
in the prefaced blood rimmed edging luminosity
of that great body of light destined to come, crowning
the primordial ritual of portents of gilded promise—
smaller dark edged bodies of light beginning to become
fully realized to me by the haunting of *Desconsado,*
a poem fulfilled with that dazed Red-tailed hawk, darting
into the safe cabin of my caffeined morning musings—

I kept scanning the shadows for feathered images diving
or even winged road-kill waving from the center strip,
ascertain that my intense depth of thoughts of them
might somehow become their conjurer, that a hot blooded
stealth of fleeting life might fulfill the outlined promises
of the ghostly figures inhabiting the passing desert vistas,
like some Saint John-like visionary auguring some wildly
dazzling taloned epiphany and behind all, I became vaguely
aware of the engine humming, a dull droning as incessant
as the hive of day-in—day-out of our lives—lives many times
wounded, don't we all wake each day with drumming blood,
with at least a tenuous feathering of the stirring of life's inherent
radiance, rising under a single golden eye, father light pluming hope—

Knowing Texas
Dave Parsons

For Roger Moore, Nancy Parsons, Cpl. Joseph D. Logan

Outside Abilene under huge sky filled fields
of the family owned cotton farm, an only son
has come back home from a life lived in
the now burn-dotted rolling verdant hill country
and the drought drudged lakes and streams
of an inexorable bustling eclectic Austin metropolis
and he is kicking the inherited dusty furrows
like the tires of some old familiar used car
with comforting boots that still fit after thirty-
some-odd years, while on the very lush edge
of the Big Thicket forest, over 400 miles southeast,
an artist is perched cozy in her small town tree
house of a studio, painting with joyful wonder
a black-capped chickadee, a bird she had never
noticed before, living cloaked for years in the deep
green shadows of lofty pines, brush, and scrub oak, while
further south, there is a man milling live oaks washed
dead with one sweep of hurricane seas gone in-
land, his ruddy hands working smooth the track
of timber destined to sail the very deadly sea
that had abruptly stopped its green prodigious
life on the Galveston strand, while further south
a padre lights candles on the altar of an old Spanish
church in Ft. Stockton, as he thinks of his own home village
thousands of miles away in India just south of Bombay,
Texas flora, fauna and people are so prodigiously
diverse that one may never live long enough
to truly know them all—this month we buried
a young Marine come home to the Sam Houston
Cemetery in Willis with only 22 years of knowing.

Offsprings of Extremes
Loretta Diane Walker

How many thousands of years have you been there?
"Questions for the Moon" by Ho Xuan Huong

321 miles west of Fort Worth
and 280 miles east of El Paso, Odessa.
How many years have you been here?
Before steel horses dipped their noses
in your trough of sand and oil?
Before obese heat sat on your days,
corpulent chills covered your nights?
Before a desiccate sky left rivers of cracks
in the belly of your red earth?

How many years have you known
the stab of cacti, brutality of wind,
conversations of coyotes,
taste of the sagebrush's bitter juice?
My body is a desert, too.
It knows the oppressive burn of want,
the cold breath that swallows bloodlines,
the cracked earth of womanhood,
the brutality of...

In the cathedral of sky,
Night, with his broad-shouldered
deep-throated darkness,
takes Moon as wife.
This is love we both understand.
Stars, like leaves, feather her full white belly
and we, orphans of day, clutch
the clipped umbilical cord hanging
in the soft birthing room of her light.

Bruised

Loretta Diane Walker

Two weeks ago, this desert West Texas town
languished, watched a bullying sun
train orange knuckles on the city.
It jabbed air— skin with temperatures
of one hundred degrees and more.
Light was hot; dust was hot; boredom was hot.

Patches of bruised yellow grass,
garden plants streaked with heat welts,
city utility workers sweat stained uniforms
were proof of brutal beating.
The wind, too lazy or scared, did not help,
wouldn't even lift its hands to blow hair.

This afternoon, when I tried to nap,
that fickle wind howled, complained,
flailed its arms at a graying sky;
windows, wind-chimes, trees trembled at this tirade.

A cavalry of heavy clouds, decked in black hats
strolled in from the east, covered the city.
Wind cowed into stillness,
sun rolled down its sleeves in defeat,
I slept, the air a sponge of cool relief,
rain—a wet gauze of healing.

Errors of the Sun
RT Castleberry

Shaking awake under sweat-heavy sheets,
I've seen sunrise eight days straight.
Aimless along the streets,
I dodge tanker trucks,
tinder of tangled trash and tree limbs,
staggered pass of cars at blank stoplights.
Braking at a brush-blinded corner,
tires slide on wood chips, dried mud.
Breakfast is fried fast food,
energy lurch of an icy Red Bull.
Slightly seedy, mostly shaved,
I shiver under restaurant air-conditioning.
Newspaper pages rattle in chapped hands.
Distractions of a book, a magazine
are open on the table.
Need narrows to thirst slaked,
four hours sound sleep.
I'm reduced to two lines of conversation.
I hold silences a little longer. I don't intrude.

A curfew cop dozes in an unlit parking lot.
I touch a cigarette to refuse below a fallen oak,
wondering if flames will speed the sun.

The House of Hours
RT Castleberry

High palms ride the wind.
High oaks shudder, shedding
leaves in the wake.
Brutalities of legacy and commerce,
eventual karma,
led to this flood-road estate,
wood and wire-trimmed paths lined
with satellite dish, children's toys, trash.
Trenchcoat tied, torn by thorns,
I surrender to unease, to bad temper's timing.
The blind man's dog barks from
a diorama of coal and cratered windows,
snarls to the end of his leash,
his laughing owner's arm.
I curse them from my doorway.
A musk of fire and chemicals masters the air.
Mimicking a movie,
the moon patches through rain layers.
Security tape slaps, clawed in a storm.
Stacked, sealed, lined in a hallway
27 boxes make a life.
I will build hours in this house through
novel's notes, photos tiled in jangled sequence,
the arcane scrutiny of a captive's language.

Debut

Kyle Schlesinger

My poetics is the hardest part. There's nothing impersonal about these poems. But that's not the hardest part. Never knew if all this noodling would amount to much, that is, until I got my big break. After I got my chops down I saw fit for appearances, but things aren't always what they seem. Poems have taught me you can just look over there at that and tell someone you trust. Catch on eventually, while all the time. Then you hit the ceiling while the sky is falling.

Other times a wink is just a blink marked by intention. I read the poems. It's morning. I used the last of the soap and went outside. I took a ride. The drugs in my mind put me at ease while the drugs in my past differentiate. My poems are sincere: it was the hardest year of my life, for me personally, to be a person. Hours pass and I collect my belongings. To a certain extent, life's all about planning for the future while being totally in the present. In the new age we'll still be skin and bones, so I hit the road. It was nice seeing you at the museum, but what I wanted more than anything was to take a swim from one end of the spring to the other. And a glass of water. You can picture it. Now turn the picture. I swam the other way. And back again.

Later I'm supposed to meet somebody somewhere. A mutual friend believe it or not. But they're not there. Danger says hello. Lately I've been having a hard time remembering people I meet in social contexts. I have a lot of anxiety in social settings, but when I get nervous I get loquacious. That's intensely personal and honest, yet professional to a degree and politically self-conscious at best, but not for lack of trying to get to the crux of what aware means and seldom.

Fact of the matter is people describe me as charming, yet colloquial and pleasant. Easy on the eyes and ears and that soothes the mind and calms the heart. Good stuff, I think to myself, and but not without an innate sense of privacy and belonging, which fits the personality. Which fits the person and the day-to-day upkeep of running around and folding things like towels and chairs, hands and arms, with an earnest sense of purpose and well-being. I know this about myself, but getting to know myself is part of the routine, like reading, meditation, and swimming. That's just for instance. Anyway, I shot some pool with your friend Tony. What a nice guy, I think to myself. Then that missing someone I mentioned earlier appears in the doorway. It was almost dusk. We made plans to take a walk but that never happened and that's worth remembering because of what I said earlier about being totally present and planning for the future. What a nice day, I think to myself later lying on the floor covered in clay. I close my eyes and read the poems, which brings me back to the hardest part.

So what do I do with my poetics? I'm working on my relic and I occasionally need poetics for it, but it's such a small amount. My consciousness as a storyteller and writer comes from the land because I am the land. I have described my poetics as a poetics of collision and as lyric conceptualism, but that won't be a thing you consider for a while. My objective in these lines is to notice the points without recognizing me in the least. I've lolled with lists that verse demands, nevertheless my ambitious plan is to improve my skills and provide you with a few bearable pieces. The instrument I am developing is a grand piano with electronic augmentations. I rolled up my sleeves after taking a seat and adapted the strings to cater to my poetics. To put it mildly, it's just twelve-tone music, but easier on the ears. Someone once said, poetry is the only means I have of saying anything positive about the world, and I think to myself, That's a sad, sad state of affairs. On a related note, I once read a slogan for an MFA program in Wyoming that claimed to be, "The last refuge for poetry," and I thought, what an awful place that must be.

My best work is occupying several dimensions simultaneously. I was talking briefly on a small panel about my poetics recently, so I had to think again about what poetics meant. It's one of those plural words that's provisional at best, a poetics of drought, an attention to what is proximal, nearby, accessible. I cannot separate my body, my identity, from my poetics, since my admiration is grounded, in part, upon a newfound interest in lyrical experimentalism. More on that later.

First, I must disclose a seismic shift in my poetics. While my poetry and prose is written without fear, my poetics is terrified, a stray fringe of woven cloth, unincorporated bits, ragged edges comprised of the phone calls I can't return, the emails that stutter, all the events that stand out without a past or a future. What I'm really talking about is interruption, the disquieting rungs of life slipping by over coffee with someone I trust.

My poetics is simple, and that's the hardest part. For example, sign and signifier are very important to me because I think we should employ the full capacity (or a limited capacity, fully) of both language and the world, like a walk with a smart dog does. The friend I mentioned earlier and I had the same political positions but our poetics were totally different. Ron Silliman critiqued my declarative categorization, calling my poetics simply transgressive, i.e., not evil in an ethical sense since these practices are representative of my poetics, a quote-unquote matter of making art out of words, because experimentation, the unequivocal personal as the political transparency of erasure, has meaning. That's all I'm really getting at: does language really need a body? One of the niceties of art is not having to say yes or no but why? I mean, the whole universe is humming, it's vibrating, and it's that hum that I want to hear. My poetics are informed by my daily psychic negotiations with culture. My new book opens with this poem:

I wanted my foot in all of them
Specifically because I like everybody
At every level there's a desire

An ancient desire of transcendence
A steppingstone in the evolution
Striving to claim some authenticity

Giving my authority to a universal
Variable where nothing stands for
Nothing other than what it is

Like in How I Got to Memphis
Patterns and colors without symmetry
If you love somebody enough

If I had to sum up my poetics in one word, it would be interiority. But we all know one word doesn't mean anything. That's why my friend from the museum and I wrote a hundred one- word poems last week. I write to prove a point to myself, but also to be quietly entertained. Poetry saves time and money. We are, almost as a reflex, destructive to the labyrinthine structure of mediation, convincing me that my poetics cannot be separated from my inability to take academics as seriously as they take themselves. But people do have ideas, like they say. Yes, people do have ideas. Deciding which books to give to the Goodwill and which books to buy and which books to read will also tell you a thing or two about what someone is made of. For example, I resolved to get rid of most of my poetry books a few years back, but I'm not naming names. Not now. When it comes down to it, my poetics seems straight forward enough. Nothing new really. I do talk a lot about such things. That's the nerves talking. There's so much great poetry in the world. More than I could read in a lifetime, which makes me wonder why anyone wants to make more of it? Maybe that's one to avoid mulling over when you're feeling blue? Maybe not. But that's beside the point.

I have been described as a late modernist, and although I'm not sure I want to be referred to as late, it's true that my poetics began with a reading of Ezra Pound, but I don't want my poems to have a uniform quality. I talk about process a lot because I'm always processing and sometimes I wish I could just turn it off and go to a canyon. I should add that I view my poetics as operating across languages. I came to believe in a poetics of mutation and then I lost my poetics somewhere along the way. In the pool or canyon or deep in meditation. Because I have a tendency toward getting to know someone with as little conversation as possible, which can come off as affection, but it's just the economy. I want a poem that's as casual as it is deep and light without catering to the usual suspects.

I'm too old to be experimental, to face the internal realities of those seduced with the jargon of condescension because it's evaporating even if you can't see it. I once wrote a poem in real time about watching a mighty river become a dreary canyon just to see if it was possible, but just as I was about to wrap it up the batteries died and I had to seek out new forms of energy, so I put five thousand years of ecological poetics into dialogue with a decade of new media poetics to see what would happen. The jury's still out on that one.

It is that, to some misleading degree, but not, entirely to my mind, in good enough keeping with the positioning of a writing desk in a public social space. When I lived in Colorado I built a desk and chair heavy enough to place in a mighty river without washing away downstream. It kept my legs cool but the poems of that period weren't so hot. It's personal, and possible to be grandiose and at times extravagant, enchanted by the irrelevant place poetry occupies in the world, but you could say that about anything.

So in conclusion, it's also worth mentioning what I've been working on in the last three weeks is a sudden and unexpected digression from the usual. Because it's current. There was nothing that needed pressing. Some people would doubtless think to call my poetics postmodern. It is that, to some misleading degree, but not, to my mind, in good enough keeping with the tradition of history. One question I'll leave you with today would thus be how to re-inscribe that older, now lost mode, the middle voice into the poem. Eventually my relationships with people and the land affected my poetics because I wanted to be astonished and atonal, so I became more experimental. It didn't last long, because I'd like to write something contingent and inductive based on a stubborn desire to put one foot in front of another to create as powerful an aesthetic experience as I can summon. Like Tom Hall said, If you love somebody enough, you'll follow wherever they go. And that's how I got to Memphis.

Barely
Nathan Brown

My car barely cuts its way
down the cattle chute of I35,

and I inhale the anonymity of it
deep into my work-stressed lungs.

I stop at that coffee shop in Waco
where young Baptist coeds huddle,

knees together and feet overlapping,
because their desire to please Christ

only barely outweighs the fierce drive
to blow some bearded religion major

who plans on becoming a preacher
after his hormones settle down a bit.

And I can barely stand my vagabond joy
for this big roll in the mud of psychosis.

J'eat Yet?
Ann Howells

Untrimmed slabs of meat ooze tomato, molasses,
and spice at Bubbaque Joe's. Sawdust on tha floor,
barnwood on tha walls, antler chan-de-liers—
and not a vegan in tha house! Jukebox plays
both country and western fer yer listenin' pleasure.
Not in a barbecue mood? Try Joe's chicken-fried steak,
chicken-fried chicken, or double-fried burgers,
sides of fried okra, fried corn, or French fries.
Craving salad? Joe recommends fried onion rings,
fried tomatoes, or his famous fried pickle
with ranch sauce. Wash it down with sweet tea
or Lone Star longnecks. Then, if yer arteries
ain't hardened past lifting fork to mouth, whistle,
and Sal'll two-step over, gum-a-poppin', pencil buried
in big hair, say *let yer belt out a notch er two,*
and take orders for fried pies: chocolate, apple,
or pecan. If tha fryer's broke, tha joint's closed.

What Kind of Animal
Ashley Smith Keyfitz

What kind of animal the joker is and whether he also smells.

What kind of lights loop the houses of the lost or serious.

That we might pour our voice, luminous & unrequested over them in the cold. Because space can be external to home & shared. Like a temporary tent made of sound and mortality. What kind of red crushes the sumac open from inside as the sun fades. No: sun sings a green against its crimson stitching. The boy said is a residue of sugar in the leaf. Paints to the dark. Who painted the bats with nail polish in the violet air. Where I was stung on the thumb by a bee & it never healed. That my hands were reverse flowers. Unblooming the air. from soil. to articulate something human. which means large enough for the biggest deaths to enter.

How I hold up my hands like holiday lights or a
sonnet to stall oil & its damage. Extinction exits like a net.

Liquid golden fossil. Deep in the quiet earth like we might erase everything for it to suck. & the note I found: "Put more goats into poems." Like a wish for healing. To run to a small farm against oblivion.

That my hands were inverse flowers. And put the peelings of root crops on our eyes to dream. You who said the flower was a wound. That feeling was a shadow of acts as they are. Met by a personal history. like the roses' crushed entrance as it takes off its jacket over & over where the tongue touches the pipeline through the river's gum. Mammal flower: twinned warmth: That we could make a hero of it. How the article said pigeons must resist misguided leaders. Who falter in the front that they must break like a wound in air. Cut the deep stitching like a rose & whether it hurts to unfurl, tiny residue of sugar that sings. so that the route made sense. But the joker wasn't an animal.

Wormwood
Michelle Hartman

If I owned Texas and Hell, I would rent Texas and live in Hell
U.S. General Philip Henry Sheridan 1866.

Landscape slowly turns on a spit suited
only for the dead, reptiles and flies dance
through cathedrals of carrion. They
are grabbed up by birds. We carved
out this land so big, made a legend
we filled with airborne coal ash, aluminum and strontium.
Air as thick as cooling cooking grease announces
more tornadoes dancing down fresh gullies
dug by recent downpours.
Arsenic, lead and radium kill lake fish
benzene and formaldehyde and uranium
sneak into our vegetables.
The drought will return,
just as floods and tropical storms
getting larger, sometimes by half.
So the governor holds prayer vigils
in convention centers.
But God, angry over abortion, not fracking,
has ruined our atmosphere.
The heavens open and rain drives
animals to line up two by two; please God,
don't save the mosquito this time. On nightly news
jackbooted floods rage into homes
and businesses. Faith healers blame
those damned gays. Large blond with three
teeth shows reporter the slab where her mobile
home use to rest. She has nothing left
except over-stuffed Hooters t-shirt,
I'm blessed, she says.
We continue to burn and slash, a Sherman's march
to economic prosperity. And Canada quietly
begins work on a big fence.

They Say the Journey is Everything
Michelle Hartman

For Nathan Brown

For Texas poets who drive
four to ten hours
to reach a town of any size
and are expected to read
     crack jokes
        and sell books on arrival,
it's more about the drinks
at the hotel bar.
As well as driving
to next reading
wearing two pairs of sunglasses
hoping no conservative decides
it's time for culture or
target practice.
Or stopping in Waco
     for double shot espresso
        chewing aspirins
and resisting urge
to strangle the Flo
who wants you
to have a Blessed Day!

The Stones of April
Bruce Bond

When the storm came, we were alone, lost
before a wall of glass, first rain, then crystal,

then stones that fell in gathering numbers,
spits of branch and shingle in the crossfire.

When the sirens sounded, we were deep
in conversation—something about your father,

how memory had left him and the scholar,
the pillar, the pacifist he was, the quiet

he kept in each home argument he suffered,
when, among the others, he was most alone.

When the end came, storms followed, wind
and the winded, tearing at their bandages,

not knowing why, everywhere the seal
of the wound broken, the fury released,

the winter stillness of the trees cast off.
It seemed so pointless, looking for the source

of all that rage, that vortex overhead,
horizontal hail that struck our headlight.

When the greater blindness came, we saw
a billion eyes come flying out of heaven,

the yard glittering in the new dark age
of clouds that swept the afternoon in legions.

We might have been strangers in the path
this late in the season, though familiar enough

the man who asks his daughter, what have you
done with my daughter. When the storm came,

we were one part wind, one part tree that gives
the wind its signature. We were the hand

that shivers in our dotage, in the wild air
that falls from nowhere, and everywhere we look.

Lakes of the Southern Plains
Bruce Bond

The numbers of the drowned are up this year.
  We know because we count them, chart them,

with or without the evidence dragged ashore.
  The numbers inside the numbers tell stories

without an end. No casket save, now
  and then, the empty box a couple lowers.

They say the majority of children wander off
  unattended five minutes or less. They say

the usual victim makes no noise, no gesture.
  They say a lot, and no one knows just why

the numbers, why these lakes in particular.
  Did the flooded trees beneath the surface

catch the swimmer unaware or breed there
  the grappling hooks of weeds among the branches.

I heard that once, and now I keep seeing
  what no one can unless, perhaps, they're drowning.

Are the depths too close, winds too strong,
  however slight the visible disturbance.

When I think of lakes of the southern plains,
  I think of stillness mostly. And yet I know

just this year a man dove in at high noon
  to get back something. Just what he lost,

the papers did not say, only that it drifted
  on the subtext of some current, unforeseen.

Farther and farther, and somewhere I imagine
  he encountered some reversal of desire,

or perhaps he had no chance, having reached
      his last stroke, his obscure object floating

over the deeper reaches, as stories do
      and those they hope to caution or reclaim.

Cross Timbers

Comancheria
Sy Hoahwah

Good-bye God, I am leaving for the Staked Plains.

It is truly a wolf's road
　　　spreading the sky open with red-stone rockets and powwows.

Bitterroot taste to the air oozing
　　　through swirling locusts.

Double-barreled sunset
　　　the ashen face

the snake emblem.
　　　There is no allegiance

even though part of my body belongs to the Comanche
　　　and part to the Arkansas River.

The rest, Coyote holds close to his heart,
　　　a handful of dirty pennies and blood pressure pills.

Night is being hauled in, piece by piece, on 18-wheelers.
　　　Owls are hooting now and the prairie is dreaming.

Dreams carve into the treetops
　　　and the black-caped numupe throws pinecones at the moon.

To sleep like this, I don't consider myself a wolf.

Choctaw Ri(gh)tes

Lydia Renfro

I'm not full-blooded; diluted one, me,
Ignorant of   ancient   memories
Shared   by my tribe.
But I know we have in us
Shilombish,   spirit,
and   *Shilup*,   shadow.
Death comes when   they both
Abandon   the body,
Vacate the fleshy   purse
and leave behind   only bone.
I'm   washed   and   laid
In temporary bed   on a scaffold,
High   up   here
I see   across the   land.
I see   Shadows
Haunting   this place,
Spirits
Walking west   to ghost lands.
And old Mother Earth   moaning,   always,
Mourning   the history she   keeps in her bosom.
They're coming   soon,
The Bone-Pickers
With long nails,   to peel away the skin
And   whatever else
Traps me in this room.
Pick it all out,   release   the big cry,
Think about   my woman   life
Until   the time   comes to take me
Into the   charnel house,
Dry,   unpigmented,   natural.

Between the Moon and Mexico
Ron Wallace

I'm looking for a day I left behind
        I'm looking for the place
where trail climbs into sky on a moonlit night
        I'm looking for the words
to a sad, old Hank Williams song,

and another summer jumps the fence.

Wild blue phlox is blooming
        round the wrought iron railing
that guards the monolithic marker
of a Choctaw chief
and the standing stones of his family
        from the meandering
of fenced cattle.

The old homeplace has fallen,
leaving only granite markers of a little cemetery
        beneath these trees
where my pony and I ride through pasture grass
in the white light of coming stars.

I haven't found the day
nor the place where trail and moon collide.
Instead I settle for blue phlox
        white stars
                and night cooled pasture grass.

I'm sure my little roan wonders
why we are here so late
        beneath a crescent moon.
He gives his reins a restless shake
as if to ask for the press of knee
        signaling time to go.
But still we pause
under night's blackened field
and listen to a whippoorwill
        sing a sad, old Hank Williams song

while September slips away on silver wisps
above rough banks that hold Red River in
    somewhere south of here
between the moon and Mexico.

Wynnewood, Nedpoint Ranch, Springtime
John Selvidge

For Skip Hill

After all this driving & even after all
        whatever years have taught us
I still remember how to cast, even
                clutch upon

    that line thrown out,
      extended either as midnight
phone call or grappling hook
    for ascent; now I trust better
its intention, pursuant of object
       laid bare & circused
by desire, how it solidifies &

compels our way, how we would
      direct ourselves that way
as colorblind pilgrims narrowing
our eyes upon the flicker of a distant
lantern. But brother, despite our victories
          we mistake

    the full spectrum of that launch for
action, velocity, trajectory, & ignore
      the slack its evacuation leaves
as ripe uncovering in us, as
    homecoming, memory beyond
        snapshot
whose gnomon casts the
      truer line—like water or

    magnetism—via the scope
of our shadows, our hungers.

    Release the hands & fall
back upon resources then. We used
to call them soul. Even in releasing
we are rich. We are still there
in every sunset, thunderstorm, every
          equine glance.

Through the Arbuckles
Carol Hamilton

Cut-away mountains so old
the upthrust of broken anticlines
stubble the hardscrabble fields
like shards of glass on Mexican fences,
reminders of our ancient brokenness,
the need for the hard-pressed to break
and finally be exposed and worn away.
The sienna and rosy stones
look hoarfrost-covered in the downpour,
though the temperature is 39°,
and the way from my house to yours
slices right through these reminders
of how young and disposable we are,
and how our moments of laughter
and chatter and just making a plan
to fill these hours together
do not count for much,
though we hold them dear.
Here the witchy fingers
of the leafless blackjack oaks
tangle the sky space
above the long-lived igneous fragments.
The seas which once lapped
the feet of these worn-to-nothing mountains
have dropped sharks' teeth
and ammonite coils all over
the dry land, and I pass by,
forget my name,
         a relic
of long-imagined importance.

Space
Carol Hamilton

We prairie-bred souls are minimalists.
I like these gelatin silver prints
of cowboys and flung-free,
parsimonious land and generous sky.
There is a day herder eating
all alone by the chuck wagon. He stands.
The cutting horse twists his body,
snaps back to the panic of the cow
that wandered away. The stray man
corkscrewed, too, to stay asaddle.
The young wranglers,
the broncobusters, the plain
cowboys live in balloons of dust,
kick earth aloft in frenzy on sight
of store or saloon. In between,
they stretch out to shoot craps,
read, make cinches, play
mumblety-peg and cards,
hear ranch boss's stories.
Skinny. They are lean, intense.
Alert as cottontail or hawk.
All attention is focused.
No waste. No rest.
This art has been cropped
close to the true composition,
the balance of bodies
against a very clean,
very distant horizon.

Behavioral Health Unit, Lawton OK
Brian Daffron

Awakened by vital checks
morning meetings
Pain level is a twelve...
Mood level is a fucking negative three...

Same scrambled egg bar as yesterday...
Nurse Ratched hands you a shot glass of pill-form joy...

One-on-one counseling sessions leave you empty.
Group therapy leaves you pissed.

A feeling of elation for craft time...GREAT!
Painting? Welding? Beadwork?
No—it's trying to weave a shitty plastic lanyard.

The best therapy
of mind and spirit
came from helping myself.

Some prayer, some writing...
some writing of prayers...
Reading Anthony Shadid weave tales
of the Iraqi civilian struggle.

Walking outside to feel the January wind
sting my face
Mount Sheridan nestled in the Wichita Mountains
looking on with indifference
but offering
comfort.

Yet even closer than Mount Sheridan—*K'op:ó:tágáu*—
is a hole
in the chain link fence
Calling my name.

Daughter, Daughter
Jason Poudrier

At three years old, you would be old enough
to represent yourself if you were in refugee court
in America, where you would be asked,
in a small, rural courtroom,
where your parents were born,
and if you would like to designate a country of removal,
and if you are afraid to go back to your home country,
and if you say no, you'll admit your deportability,
daughter.

Daughter, at six years old,
you will be old enough to have been shot
at a school in America.
At seven years old,
in another nation,
and in some close-distant parts of America,
you will be old enough to start being trained
to kill, by killing small animals.
The rat found in the chicken coop,
the chickens, when their breasts are full,
stringing them upside down on a clothesline,
cutting slits on each side of their throats,
letting their blood flow out,
then boiling and plucking the feathers.

At nine, daughter, you would be ready to kill
the goat you raised. It would look at you
with its rectangular pupils,
and your knife-bearing hand
would pull across its throat.
You'd learn to hang it, skin it,
clean out the organs,
separate bone from meat,
cutting through cartilage
with a paring knife.

At ten, daughter,
in parts of Africa and the Middle East,

where Americans have sold weapons,
deployed soldiers, found oil, diamond mines or gold,
you would be old enough to be proficient
in taking apart, cleaning, and putting together an AK-47.
You would know how to load a magazine,
your fingers sore at first from depressing
one round after the other into a thirty-round
banana-curved magazine. You would race against your peers,
be able to load a magazine in under thirty seconds.
You would know how to slap it into the stock,
pull back the bolt, switch the safety switch to fire,
and be ready to kill, ingrained with ideas
that there are values greater than the value of life.
Old enough to be a leader in a child army,
taking care of the young,
teaching them to take care of each other,
take apart, put together an AK,
kill for one another, or kill one another.

At age twelve, if not younger,
in other nations, or even in America with parental consent,
you will be old enough to be a bride,
or straight up sold for sex.
You could be kidnapped, raped, impregnated
with a child that you would love because it is yours
and hate because it reminds you of him, of then,
and when rescued after years of enslavement,
you would wonder where your life went.

At age sixteen, daughter,
in America, you could kill a man
in attempt to escape from being trafficked for sex
or as a way to escape an unwanted marriage,
but you would be found guilty
because the prosecution would be able to prove
premeditation, and you would face life in prison.

But right now daughter, you are my daughter.
Your mom labored for nine hours
under the care of a midwife, without medication,

because your mom feared drugs more than pain.
When you turned one, you walked
because the dress we put on you for your birthday
was too hard to crawl in, getting stuck under your knees.
At two you could scroll through pictures on my iPhone
and find the ones you liked, of you, as a baby.

At age three, daughter,
you learned to do forward rolls
at a place called Tumble Time
in a strip mall in Oklahoma.
At age four, you started preschool
and began to recognize letters,
first identifying beginning letter sounds,
then reading your first words,
Cat, hat, rat, sat, bat.
And I want you to know, daughter,
to learn, daughter, about the world.
You can make a difference, daughter.
Your voice matters, daughter.

Love Poem to a Perfect Stranger
Jason Poudrier

I am eating ramen while I write this poem.
I used spell check to spell pretentious,
and poetry is supposed to be sparse and meaningful,
and I have just burnt three lines,
but I just wanted to tell you,
the world would not be complete without you;
I should show not tell, I know,
and it sounds hyperbolic, but it's true.

You may not always make honest decisions,
like me—on the way home I got pulled over
for speeding. Before the cop got out of his car,
I turned the radio to the Christian station
and turned up the volume. I was in Oklahoma.
It was a small town. I didn't want a ticket.

I am just trying to relate.
Maybe you are innocent.
I once thought that about myself,
but then I was born and learned to think
and became aware of my extremities,
cheated on my girlfriend in middle school.
Go Tigers.

Know that I love you.
I know we've just met,
well not really met,
but you're reading this poem, and I wrote it.

Maybe I will be dead and buried
in a cemetery in a small town
you've never heard of with a generic name,
like Rush Springs, Oklahoma,
and because we never met,
this poem will be the only thing
that bridges the distance of space and time
and connects us forever,

until you die, or until you forget,
that you read a poem one day
written by someone you never met
who loved you.

Red Fields
Jason Poudrier

My feet sink into the soil
of my father-in-law's
Oklahoma land,
reminding me of times
before I met his daughter,
when I drove along
in a tank convoy
towards Baghdad
at the same
pace as a tractor
over an unplowed field.

With each stop,
we would have fifteen minutes
to dig two foxholes,
with e-tools
better designed for
digging 1'x 1' cat-holes.

When the sand was soft
like the overworked edges
of the short rows
of my father-in-law's fields,
it was a blessing.
We'd dig our holes deep,
safe, to plant ourselves into
if we came under fire,
so we could rise out
when the lead rain ended.

When the sand was as hard
as the unworked ground
hiding under the buffalo grass,
our e-tools would chink
at the surface with every hit;
our holes would be shallow,
and we'd push the sand up
around the perimeter,

making a false reservoir of safety,
knowing bullets would penetrate
the powdered walls if we were ambushed,
and our bodies would lie half-exposed
in shallow graves, in pools
coloring the sand Oklahoma clay.
When his daughter was only
a pin-up girl in my mind,
the sandstorms would erase
the foxholes after we pushed forward;
now I drive my father-in-law's tractor
and set the plow into the soil
to cultivate his land.

Dream Song Delta 1-39
Jason Poudrier

Blind dog staccato howls
in regular intervals in four-four time,
on guard like me, can't sleep.
Am I happier here?
When in we talked like cellmates,
"How many years you got?"
Wife alongside, "Wish that damned dog'd
shut the hell up and you'd quit movin' around."
Her warm body lets me know
I'm back, in a bed, no chance
of hearing howling desert collies
or stuttering radio static, while waiting for word,
watching for movement,
watching meteor-bright rounds
break silence and darkness,
creating momentary, blinding black
before eyes realign and rockets
shell the distance in a pop-and-flash,
like dry Oklahoma thunderstorms
casting repeated shrouded lights
through wooden window blinds.
Sitting-up-sleep, head resting
on a salt-stained, flack-vest pillow,
visions cast of wife, son, daughter,
causing gloved fingers to curl
around cool eighty-degree air,
pang of home up in a pop,
a flash on the horizon.
Am I,
am I happier here?

At the Okie Noodling Festival
Nathan Brown

Once we exited off I-35 and turned
toward Pauls Valley, we just followed
the big black or red and raised pickups
with four-foot wheels n' beer coolers
slidin' around in their rusty beds.

We couldn't park down in the drainage
ditches where they did, but the curb
on Chickasaw Street worked fine
for our city-shit Honda Accord.

The band that my friend Charley
threw together for the big event
was putting the finishing touches
on "Freebird," with the distortion

cranked up, as we walked into the ill-
defined edges of a scene that would,
betcha ten bucks, make some cocky
New Yorker wet his fancy trousers.

Not that anyone would've noticed,
since it was 106° in the damn shade
of the oaks and dried up elms where
fans n' noodlers alike crammed in to

escape the teeth of a July sun. So,
most ever'body's trousers were
already moist—like the grass
was a dead gray and floatin'

around in the air with the dirt,
the dust and the damn chiggers
stirred up by all the got-dang
goat-raper-shit-kicker boots.

Knee Deep in October
Cullen Whisenhunt

And what did I learn, wading
      the river in cool fall evening?
What, after wandering down worn sandstone steps?
      What, while tracing Tishomingo's trails?

I learned of sand, sharp with shell and gravel,
      of rocks, smooth and grey and gorgeous,
and I learned the green of fall that drips
      from vines and branches and collects
as algae, in pools where caves sprout from under dead logs.

As fresh-fallen dam water pushed each footfall
      further sideways, I wanted it to make meaning,
to be a metaphor for me and my work and the rushing
      of time like leaves on the wind or twigs in the water.

But, it was just the river—the creek, actually—and even then
      too wide and winding to mind my wishes.

Earth Mover
Laura Da'

Ferocious and sly, my mind's talon
plucks liquid movements from rivers,

arteries, ink, amniotic fluid, delicate webs of optical nerves.
Puckered prospect of the Cesarean veil.

My skin twisted in stainless steel pliers proves
the efficacy of the spinal block that dulls

my pain but leaves a cavity for the sonic panic
of my child heaved from my abdomen.

I close my eyes and roll hills,
churn rivers, press shovel to earth and brace

for the abrasion that draws the past
glistening into the present.

In the Ohio Valley, mound builders
left massive earthworks.

Enamored with the idea of excavation,
settlers pilfered through the soil,

sorted remnants: feather headdresses, flakes of mica, pot shards,
bone fragments. When asked to define

an effigy depicted in a perplexing mound—
The Shawnee described *a perilous being wrought*

like a massive panther swimming
through rivers with the power to destroy and renew.

Alligator mound.
No.

I net the past and future in panther skin.
My son's ferocious cry—fanged and clawed

grip on the skin of the toppling world. I clamp down
on the tributary's gush, lay claim to our place here.

Fishing in the Family Pond in Wilburton
Logan White-Mulcare

Where the water
Meets the grass,
Just after the mud,
There, sitting,
Dreaming,
Drinking
In that
Heat.

That sound,
Like the most
Precious machine,
Pulsing with the sun,
Out from the trees
Down
To the water,
Starting small like
Ripples,
Growing,
Edging out into silence
Until the next rise
And eventual fall.

Learned a lot fishing,
from the pond,
from the machine of bugs
and waves
and pine needles
twisting, by breeze,
into each other,
Drinking in the
Breeze,
Waking,
Standing
In the place
Where the grass
Meets the water
Just before
The
Mud

Native American Day
Ricco Wright

it's a CRYING sham(e),

like the Trail of Tears

in the 19th century,

that we're

in the 21st and

~~Columbus Day~~ "Columbine Us Day"

is a *federal* holiday

in /əˈmɛɹɪkə/ and

Native **American** **Day** ain't

Indian Meridian
Allison Adelle Hedge Coke

Over Coffee Creek, along the meridian,
we ruptured earth in the drive, driven by some compulsion,
found the femur, then knew. The tarantulas were black that summer
ranging the road at night in a time they should have slept.
Morning, the swish swish of rattlers, like sprinklers,
letting everyone know their migration was in. Fire ants, creepers.
Yet, everything was fine, till the tornados hit.
Till the dance was day to day and the stray came
one evening, until the strangers brought that Gypsy
Varner stud and dropped him in the pasture without
a bit of care for my mare, forget the gelding. In
the midst of storms we loaded them up and moved
up the road, starting over. Definitely not the way those
folks had done when they sounded the call to rush
and ran all over the place staking claims, we had none,
wanted none and were just there to stay a while, like
the twisters, really. Like the skirted storms shaking snakes,
and horses until night and day all dream in green and the weather
waves itself goodbye.

Blessing
Josh Wann

god bless the children
whose daddies like bourbon and
slide guitar too much.

god bless the little children
whose daddies know the turnpike
better than their own beds.

god would you please bless the children
whose socks get sticky burrs all over
when lookin' for food.

god also don't forget to bless the children
whose mommas are trusting the TV to watch the kids while they
clock-in again and again and again.

god, if it's not too much trouble, bless the children
whose mommas throw the groceries in the floorboard of the truck
        and curse when the cans fall
out.

god, sorry to bother you again, but bless the children
who, to keep from talking to themselves, make friends with the
        cattle and the trees
while no one else is home.

god, I won't come around again, but bless the children
who know the court summons, the disconnect notice, and the junk mail
all go in the same pile.

And I'll get out of your hair now, but god bless the children
who are understanding these blessings now that they ain't children

and got children of their own.

Red Rock Canyon
Josh Wann

there are still places in Oklahoma
where you don't have to pick up
travel brochures because you are
making the dogged rasping history.

between Nancy's Lighthouse and
Ann's Fry House you can hear the
music of turnpike semis shuffling
their tires between weigh stations
and stars on the plains highways.

learn the language of women made
wise by Old Crow, cigarettes, and
ex-husbands smart enough to know
none of these things bring wisdom

and that wisdom is, in fact, a lie
trickster word woven and spun
by the elderly to sell to young folk
convincing them and themselves

that old age has something /oh god
it's got to be something/ if you mash
and distill and compost your moments
into a string of words to give young folk

who right now are busying themselves
with scraping together potluck beer
money and forging for bare armed hugs
to keep warm /and anything but alone/

hoping that one day if they don't
stumble gun into the sky spirit
they'll come out of the woods and
repeat what the fire taught them.

English Second Language Classes
Johnny Catfish Mahan

LESSON #1
Practical Definitions in Context:

I pledge allegiance
(Pledge; same as promise, kind of like swear)
[Promise; saying to be trusted. {promises are meant to be broken}]
(Swear; to curse, i.e. as in Paco, you swear a lot.)

to the flag of the United States
(United; together like family, special note; words used as proper names don't necessarily retain original meanings.)
(States; area of landmass drawn on maps inside country drawn on maps. Mode of thought or frame of mind. [State can be used to say "I'm in Idaho, or I'm in denial.])

of America
(America; not all of North America, but just their part of it as outlined on maps.)

and to the Republic
(Republic; see Roman Empire.)

for which it stands
(Stands; stand can mean like stand on the corner and look for work, but here it means more like Stand Behind, or Backup your people, Stand up for each other, but not as in this is all I can stand.)

one nation under God
(One; singular unit as in uno, not no more. [However, this does not count or take into consideration Native Americans and their nations within the US.])
(Under; beneath, below, less than, dependent to ...)
(God; ?, The Supreme Court is still considering the nation's stance on this one.)

indivisible with
(Indivisible; not divided, ?, see United, perhaps. In division within itself?)

Liberty and Justice
(Liberty; A lady statue in New York City, a bell in Philadelphia, Pa, a tree somewhere back East. A sailor's holiday. Something supposedly equal to dying, i.e. "Give me Liberty or give me Death.")
(Justice; really good cowboy boots. Justin Timberlake's real first name. Also, some term they throw around in law courts.)

for all.
(All; every one of them who have it already, but not for anyone needing this class.)

This is One of the Nine Wide Worlds, and the Creatures that Inhabit it Lull

Stacy Kidd

First of all, it isn't tenderhearted.
Boys are as small
as their fathers' fingers, their tongues stained
with wild plum, their faces—vapid
little things all the way from West Texas,
a place even wilder than this
wind where the river appears
only an inch deep. If you look
near the surface, the boys
might betray light that leans in
from backwoods for a can of snuff
or stick of black-jack if
that's all you have. They'll tell you
about the calf cut last December
from the ice, but in the case
of their own lives, they'll grow quiet,
and the quiet will grow like nails
from the tips of their fingers,
and the stillness will scratch at anything.

bark

Stacy Kidd

1.

What can carry story can hold old
to our borrowed grammars—

a boy might burrow his head
into a pillow, into an after

thought or what we say to him when

we don't follow him, or pray for him,
we articulate exactly this

way. What can move once can stagnate.

The lake, right there the lake—
we can see living

trees in the water.

2.

A boy for the day and not the night, a boy
like kindling—he wrecks

what he will. He travels
a lake and a dog fetches water.

The lake, like a family, sits
plenty and pretty becomes a kind

apparition—we think
in parentheses, in uses. Two

hands turned against what is shown,
a boy necks his way

into a wood, always leading. He blinks
with important decisions.

We know how to make him certain.

3.

Say, again, the boy & note his affection.

Stillwater is lit in lakes & will not drown.

A movie, maybe, a movie has started

to etch. All the boys & their still frames.

Each incision, a precision in crops.

Call it an ace out of acre.

Say the boy walks a lake & signed bricks

are built into old decks & footpaths,

are a litany of we.

4.

Nothing is moving here

We can sing into this hymnal

We can carve out a space, can say
a boy carves out a space, we can say

"hah"

Turnpike // Ghost

Hala Alyan

Wrong morning, late train, I was wearing red for you.
A girl-thief. Startled,

the train lurched between two smokestack towns.
The subway, eye of a concrete needle.

Orchids, purple-furred. Trashed along with the orange peels.
Tulip-wearer. I never understood Brooklyn,

how a place could be bigger than it was.
The bartenders ask if I want another before I've had a first.

You, forest-eyed, a lake in the pocket of your khakis. I launder,
fold the warm clothes,

find a porch inside them. You call me home. Home.
What an Oklahoman sky is made of:

arrow in red dirt, quilt in the home team's colors.
Chimes to announce the wind.

My father wanted a suburban lawn. Warm biscuits at Red Lobster.
He knows America as equations to be memorized:

ghost + furniture + eastern turnpikes. Fog as home.
The expressway, congested with commuters,

cars that steer back the way they came. I never did learn to drive.
Even if I wanted to leave, I couldn't.

1999

Hala Alyan

I had never seen true desert before: cactus beds and milk-white sand, sand that ran for days, the lipstick-red of dusk. There I was, digging through piles of library books to steal the best ones, lumping my bedsheets into a mouth to kiss. I wasn't quick enough to stop the boy's hand under my shirt. I starved myself to starve my mother. In that house we made a house for each of us, the corn fields a row of brunettes after the winter drought. In ten years, a man will fall in love because he recognizes the Midwest in me. He will leave a note in the pleat of my coat. When the final box was taped up, my father eyed the house once before turning back towards the Dodge, destined to do it all over again.

~

I had lived in a desert before; I did. I forgot the za'atar my mother said she fed me in Iraq. I forgot my grandmother's house in Soo-ree-yaa. There I was, eating the prickly pears even though they always made my tongue itch. A teacher in Texas told me I'd never learn how to pronounce my own name in English and she was right. I wept until my mother took me to McDonald's. In that house I was the only child. I danced in the hot winter. In ten years, a boy will leave marks on my arm because I call him a redneck. I stole a Barbie pink windbreaker from the cubbyhole at school. There was nothing in the pockets. Even before the sun rose, my father went outside to smoke and watch the birds fly east. He loved the ugly ones best of all.

Portrait
Paul Austin

For Richard Ray Whitman

his face
lines
furrows
maps
stories
mysteries
from way back

his words
few
spoken soft
leave
spaces
to listen
for unheard songs

his eyes
amused
surprised
by wisdom
amazed
to have made
the journey
still standing

his walk
noiseless
of no
disturbance
a presence
a needed
reminder

himself
the poem

Will Rogers Turnpike
Quraysh Ali Lansana

these roads my veins   dry red
clay body sun smoke wafts heat
tired of itself wheezing semi-trailers
alfalfa between cheek and gum

cicada guitar twang ditties tink
powerline towers alien horizon
march shoulders hawk respite
in absence of elm and birch

dust devils square dance prairie
as Christian clouds loft fervor
sun to our right   only sky blue
this land our road hum and scent

something dead every quarter mile
what are you, Mexican? the kind cracker
asks at truck stop   amazed to learn
of duet between nelly and tim mcgraw

patience is the I-35 junction abrupt
urban merger night a blindfold
headlights on city
licks chops and growls

Horticulture
Brent Newsom

Mid-June, a gangly, wide-eyed eight-year-old
with pinkish, peach-fuzzed Dumbo ears
oversoaped the dishes his first night,
deliberately, gleeful as soapsuds spewed
from the Kenmore onto the kitchen tiles.
I went for the mop while, firm but calm,
the Director sent the boy to bed, which he also wet
deliberately.   I didn't go home that college summer
but part-timed as a nursery vendor
at a big-box lawn and garden center—
made "color" the first thing "guests" would see,
trimmed leaves gone brown with drought or disease—
and interned at the ranch for troubled boys,
hired-hand-slash-babysitter (*Role model,*
the Director said, *A presence*)
with a furnished, private room, rent-free.
Discipline was not in the intern's job description,
so Dumbo clipped my heels, yakking with candor
while I pulled squash and young cucumber
or set an iron fencepost, pretended to listen,
which should have been enough. A presence.

He felt so deeply I felt embarrassed
when he spoke of why his mother left him
with grandparents (now I can't recall—
the psych ward, drug habit, jail?)
and of why his grandma and grandpa left him
with us. *It made me hurt inside,*
he said, *but I know they're too old
to keep a kid.* He was wiser in that way,
and more mature, than I, unacquainted
with such frankness and such grief.

But on the ranch's hard red dirt, tenderness
was taboo. Ten feet up the climbing wall,
he screamed. The others jeered as he clung

too stiffly, then slipped. He wailed,
knowing only the rope I held
saved him from falling. He'd felt those lines
go slack before. His dusty sneakers strained
for solid ground, and when they touched
he clung to my waist, rivulets on his dirty cheeks,
snot quivering on his upper lip. He needed
more than I knew how to give.

I volunteered for extra hours at work,
preferred to pluck dead blades from sprays
of purple fountain grass, arrange displays
of garish zinnias, set pallets of young crepe myrtles
outside the gate. I lined up pots of hostas
straight as rails in a white pipe fence,
napped on patio chairs whenever I could.
Evenings, I unrolled a rubber hose,
gave everything another splash of water.
The caladiums leaned toward me, giant
green-veined ears eavesdropping on my prayers
for autumn.
          By August he was gone;
but I still felt the weight of him, hanging
in mid-air by the rope that linked our bodies
like an umbilical cord, still heard his voice
grow shrill and dry before I let him down.

Oklahoma Haibun
Sharon Martin

Was it three or four years ago that the drought first dried up the creek? It was the summer that the okra blossoms burned up and dropped off, when my harvest was nothing but peppers and eggplant. I don't like eggplant. Last summer, it was cool here, but blistering in Seattle. This year, I let the garden go. I planted and watered, but I didn't weed. Volunteers took up whole patches. The bees, the birds, and the butterflies loved the lemon balm, the four-feet-tall marigolds, chickweed and Malabar spinach. I got a few potatoes, some early tomatoes, but then the petunias and the tomatoes burned up. I made note of what survived— vincas, cannas, those peppers again. There was still color, still food for frogs and rabbits. In the face of uncertainty, I'll call that success.

> My senator knows
> Earth is not getting warmer.
> His proof? A snowball.

Moments after Murrah
Catherine Katey Johnson

Violence reclaims our days.
My wedding anniversary,
a time of something old and borrowed,
then something new blew up
a bellow in my ears,
doors burst open
in our place, fifteen miles away.

Moments after Murrah's dark fog lifted
standing there
were the south and west two-thirds of it
and a hole, a hand-blown bowl of dust,
debris and truck parts
raining for three blocks,
fiery foreign cars,
two hundred buildings
that used to have windows to—
    LOOK OUT!—
My friend was minutes late to work and alive
while co-workers joined the others
 whose time cards held nine, oh, two—
punched out by the dozens
sent to bits by a Ryder.

If you had only parked there this morning,
or we had all circled it
with our Wagoneers, Escorts, and Mavericks;
if others had parked there instead,
to attend the free government
sponsored seminars
about pensions,
or how to buy a license to deal
arms
and legs
hands
in the concrete
pancaked over day care
Social Security,

Customs,
Housing,
Urban Development
nearly five on the Richter,

a thousand men and women
wouldn't keep sifting
round-the-clock evidence
and babies wouldn't lie
on park bench
make-shift
morgues.
~~~~~~

"Moments after Murrah," mentioned in *The New York Times*, June 24, 1995.

Untitled
Sandra Soli

flash of panic
as I reach the underpass
Ryder truck above

Triweekly Cimarron River Report, May 17th to August 28th

Timothy Bradford

High and tumultuous, medium and running, *dulce et decorum nella sulla bankula*, ethereal and brown, murky but clearer than the North Canadian Cimarron red, frothy and shimmering, vaguely blue, silvery and verdant, pensively dark green, aqua sienna, milk teeth blue, frothy and stringy red, khaki, pimento and bass, greyhound green, crimson but given to viridescence, lapis lazuli, steel brown, interstate blue, shimmering taupe, recycled white glass, slate, macadam, invisible, tree bark, shivering liver, *café au lait*, minnow, chiffon, raspberry margarita, month-old caramel apple, lady of the lake green and silver, manure, milky vermeil, catfish belly and roiling, invisible, brick house, Serengeti red, gravy spleen, cattle, basalt.

Transformers
Timothy Bradford

It's on, now
    happening here, God, or Nature,
        cows in the field, uniform
        and coloring.

    A Transformer is both
        a jet and a robot, a car
and a robot. Some are called

Decepticons, but they really should be called
        Realityicons. Everything is
something and something else then
        something else again.   You are still you

sort of, your body transformed
        but we're glad you're still
in it.   And you are you as we learn
        who you are.   And   four comes
      before five   most of the time.

On the growth chart, who's to say
        what height you should   be at
        when you're God,   or Nature.

Everything all at once
        streaming out of the goddess's
    yoni. The boy said over dinner,

        "I like to call people   twats
    because it's not so offensive."
        (He meant twits.)

God, or Nature,   is   shining down
        upon us,   making
a road to drive on   and is
        driving the atmosphere
    round.   Trees stand by, are good for

many things. Their puissance is
        enormous and deceptive. We

        breathe   it in.

Between Okemah and Okmulgee County
Jane Taylor

We were headed to Okemah. Suddenly, we appeared to be in a place called Henryetta. We got out to get our bearings and to look at the Okmulgee county rodeo posters. Downtown was mostly boarded up. We stretched and wandered up and down the blocks. There is a name for those weeds that bloom in broken sidewalks, but neither of us could remember it. Then, look there. A tidy sign painted over storefront glass. *House of Overalls*. Inside, nothing but racks. Every style: striped, corduroy, denim, suede-ish, tan-ish, camo, even toddler camo. All the nubs, buttons and fasteners gleamed. I beheld every kind of hardily stitched loop and hammer holder. I was taken back. I never see an overall without remembering my dad, the telephone man, a union guy, hanging diapers on the line, clothespins clipped to his bib like wooden birds. He whistled across the yard while mother put my baby brother to sleep with Frank Sinatra on the radio. Out of this scrap of memory, this pocket of nostalgia, I would have bought myself a pair of Oshkosh, but, darn it, the amazing *House of Overalls* was open only by appointment, and we had to turn around and go back to the proper exit for the Woody Fest in time for Arlo.

Río de los Carneros Cimarrón
Jeanetta Calhoun Mish

In Osage country, a river of many names—
Red Fork, Grand Saline, Newsewtonga,
born on a mesa near Folsom, New Mexico
where ancient ones chipped history onto projectile
points, lived amid juniper, ponderosa, and piñon
among brooding volcanoes humped on horizon.

The River of Wild Sheep carves its way
through canyon's gray porphyry palisades,
contests four states' lonely hoodooed borders.

Near Black Mesa where dinosaurs stomped
their feet, where bighorn and antelope graze
shortgrass prairie and bears scratch winter-
weary backs on petrified trees, where shards
of the universe encased in cimmerian silk
glint and glitter, sky-road bright as a turnpike,
the river turns north, hides in its silty channel.

Returning dry and thirsty from its Kansas foray,
the Cimarron southeasts into Oklahoma where
it loans its broad banks to the town of Freedom.

Downstream, its spiced-cider flow drinks from Eagle
Chief and Skeleton Creeks, where few remaining
stands of little bluestem and panic grass reclaim
once-cultivated fields, surrounding ramshackle barns,
singing with the wind in an old prairie dialect,
waving at a pair of bald eagles circling prey.

Below confluence with the Arkansas its wild flow
now dammed into Keystone Lake to host genteel
picnics and regattas—escaping over the weir

El Río promises its stories to the Mississippi.

Prairie Metaphysics
Don Stinson

The roads here are so straight
you expect to keep going forever
until you see distant water
and drive to another continent
somewhere far, far away.

Everything is straight lines,
everything is horizon.
It's no wonder people here
think the way they do,
as if all is linear.

But often, in the distance—
perhaps clouds or
some grey sort of haze
over the horizon,
a sense of uncertainty,

a question mark
suspended over the prairie,
and it's all an illusion,
nothing is really straight,
but a subtle, so subtle curve,

and eventually I'll drive to
simply more prairie,
arrive back at the very
same place: the period
under the curve.

I Shalopy Moo
Paul Bowers

They are like trees, planted by streams of water.
                                    Psalm 1:3

Marched to in Selma, Alabama,
a sing-along with M.L. King
crossing the Edmund Pettus Bridge,

then Pete Seeger and Joe Glazer's version
singing for the Union—

We shall not be moved.

Played as a team chant
for the Leicester City Football Club
when it takes the field at King Power Stadium

and the walk-on song
for Shirley Crabtree
aka Big Daddy, the British grappler,
before a heavyweight wrestling match
against Giant Haystacks—

We shall not be,
we shall not be moved.

Closer to the heart
is Mississippi John Hurt
with his Delta blues guitar—

I shall not be moved

and Johnny and June
with a lively beat and tambourine—

Just like a tree planted by the waters

and my six-year-old sister
in Sapulpa, Oklahoma,

Emmanuel Missionary Baptist Church,
sometime in the mid-70s
testifying with odd
fruits of the spirit—

I shalopy, I shalopy moo.
I shalopy, I shalopy moo.

We confessed to one another at late Sunday supper
how such childish errors surely forced a smile
on the suffering criminal grimace of Jesus,
saved him from that silly burden of perfection,
his thirst quenched by a hymn of made-up words.

An Oklahoma Weather Poem that Makes No Mention of Tornadoes

Paul Bowers

In the rural wilds
the wind drives life away

by the fistful
by the dustful
by the leaful.

We are graveled
and wind groomed
cow blustered, horse gusted.

Know that our limbs bend,
manes twist,
dirt mangles;

know that the air
weaves and unravels
makes porch pots shatter.

The bob and wheel
of air moves us,
lifts us, rhythms us,

rhymes us. Who could live
in stillness, plainless
sweepless

without the bloom of a dirty sun
the angled stab in February
or the hot bent flame of June?

The Last Chance
Jim Barnes

At Lester's Place. Talihina. 1964.

The myna bird speaks
of love. His whistle
cuts into the bone
ears of a whitetail's
head stuffed above
the bar.

Fifty miles, the county's
dry. You stop here
to tell yourself
go home, but hear
the black experience
of a goddamned bird

whose hello sucks
at the marrow
of your bones.
You wonder how a soul
can pass from
his beak and break

upon your face, split
the whiskers you grew
to be wise in. You wonder
at his avalanche of words,
the last drink you took,
the dance on your skin

you can't beat time to.
You wonder, but you
do not ask. You
listen hard with
your cracking eyes.
He asks about your life.

You tell him lies
while he prunes
a feather, lets it drop.
Your life is sour
in the glass. Crow
made the earth and all

things therein, brought fire.
This bird's a ghost
you tell your sins.
Nobody is listening.
Outside, the sun falls
into the brittle grass.

Touching the Rattlesnake
Jim Barnes

The neighbor's leg was black from toe to thigh,
with yellow pus oozing from cuts he'd made
trying to stop the poison from reaching
his heart. He showed the three of us stumbling
into his house, after Sunday school set
us free, what he said we would be afraid
to see. The swollen blackness made me shudder
with adolescent sins I knew we were doomed
to hell for. He dared us to touch the leg.

Tight as the shell of a dried gourd, the skin
seemed to break with each slight movement he made.
I left with the smell of venom in my lungs,
my eyes careful with every rock we passed
on the way to the swimming hole. I lay
on the shoal and felt the current crawl along
my body until all thought of fangs were washed
away and the rattle of leaves above my head
seemed only leaves. *Amazing grace, how sweet*

I sang straight up into the Sunday sky.
The others splashed my face, and we wallowed
like carp in the mud. We could not know that one
of us would die before the sun went down, fangs
buried in his neck as he reached over a boulder
to pull himself up the face of the cliff above
the swimming hole. Nor that he would live just
long enough to climb back down, boasting that
he touched the snake before it struck his neck.

The neighbor did not die, but thrived on guts
he said it took to have a snaky leg.
I could not forget the oozing blackness
and never crossed his door again, nor how
white the naked body of my friend lay.
The wind rose late that day and made the limbs
crash above our heads. That night it rained.
The sound of thunder and shotguns carried us
through a domain of snakes we would annihilate.

After the Great Plains
Jim Barnes

Nothing remains the same in this long land.
Bird, fox, gully, grass, all are history
as soon as the moon rises or the wind climbs,
tales told by shadows leaning toward a vista
few eyes discern.

What strikes the windshield hardest as you drive
across is haze, distance claiming being
as absolute as the grasshoppers crushed on
the glass. There is no sameness to a land
that paints itself

different each dawn. The wind in your hair
today becomes a mouse's breath four states
beyond tomorrow. The river you ford could not
be any river. Particular, it flows through
the heart of the land.

After the Great Plains you are not the same.
No matter which way you cross something stays
firmly with you, a sense hard to name, like
a pebble in the toe of your boot you can't shake
out in this life.

The Child from the Well
Jessica Isaacs

A Retelling of an Archetypal Folktale

The child came up out of the well; usually, children fell in and were gone forever, but this time, the child came up from the watery below and leaked into all of their lives, cried
"water, give me water,"

and what mother, what grandmother, could deny any babe a cool drink? cried "meat, give me meat," whispered Mamma so softly that every mother ached to claim this one as her own,

so the women cried to their husbands and fathers, they cried to their brothers and uncles to hunt, and the child ate. The child ate and the men hunted, until the child grew thirsty again and cried, "water, give me water,"

so the women drew more water from the well, and the child drank until there was no more water to be drawn. Still, the child cried, "more, mamma, more,"

so the women went to the river with their pails, they carried pail after pail of river to the child, and the child drank the river, yet still the child thirsted, "mamma," the child whispered,
"water, give me water,"

so the women went to the lake with their pails, they carried pail af-ter pail of lake to the child; the child drank the lake, and the village children shriveled into dried skins, until one by one they died, save the child from the well, who cried, "mamma, give me more,"

so the mothers went to the ocean, and the child drank the ocean, but the salt burned and the child cried, "water, give me water,"

so the mothers went to the clouds, riding the men's arrows, they brought down the rain, and the child drank the rain, yet still the child thirsted, cried, "more, mamma, more,"

and since no more children lived, the child nursed the mothers'
milk, and since the men had no milk, the child drank the men's
blood, yet still the child thirsted, cried, "more, mamma, more,"

so the mothers went to their kitchens, they gathered their sharpest
knives, they gathered together, with knives and pails at the well,
raised knives to wrists, slit their veins, filled pail after pail, to-
gether, filled the well from which the child came, and the mothers
cried, together,
"water, give me water."

Tender of Flesh
Jessica Isaacs

Their machines are bigger than us, and they push harder
than our tender bodies know how to push—we who are
but flesh and blood, ground into the earth by their brute force,
their artificial strength mocking the strength we carry
in our words and our mere hands—we who are
organic, like the sands of the Canadian River bed, a mighty river,
yet unable to defend itself against the industrial progress
of workers arriving in droves like a legion of demons,
glittering like money in their lines of RVs,
spinning promises like the Pied Piper, exploiting our years
of poverty and desperation, buying our loyalty, our land,
our water, our children's years.

When we first heard they were coming,
we tried to speak for the River, who could not speak
for itself. We said to the workers, please,
don't come through here. We said,
you must be men and women of reason. We said, please,
listen to us.

But they would not listen. They could not hear
over their machines. So we spoke louder;
we shouted over their clamor. We said,
sometimes life is more important than money. We said,
don't take advantage of us because we are poor,
don't roll right over us because you can,
because we aren't made of steel and fuel.We said, please,
don't patronize our desperation with your economic double-talk,
please, please, please–

But they answered with their machines, rolling over all of us,
human and river, blood and clay,
grinding us deeper into the battered earth, reminding us
that steel is bigger than flesh, that industry is mightier than earth,
that they are stronger than a simple drop of water,
that they are the winners in the courts, the holders of the law–

and we who wish only to protect our rivers,
our earth, our way of life – we who are
pushed aside by brute force because we who are

weaker than steel—we are the losers to these machines
fueled by immense greed for more jobs for more masses, more
manufacturing for more money, more transporting for more
tar sands and poison across the countryside,
through our ancient aquifers, shattering the very ground
our children run and laugh and grow on—we can do Nothing,

but cry out for awareness—we can do Nothing,
but chain our tender flesh to cold steel—we can do Nothing,
but warn our children what lies beneath the surface—
what demons of efficiency course through the clay
beneath the seemingly innocent pastures of plenty.

And we who are
but flesh and blood—we who are
but water and clay—we who are
strong in spirit but tender of flesh—

we can do Nothing,

but teach our children to listen.

Lost Weekend in Tonkawa
John Selvidge

raise a glass (but not
too full) to the in-between
times. Odds are this motel's
varmint-free but let's sleep

above the covers & wear shoes
into the bathroom. So much space
in this bed, always space in bed
now, less space in the head so

the air conditioner's all the music
I need. Alone has its heights &
depths, each personal pronoun's like
a fuse following its incendiary train

from *she* to *him* to *I, I, I* to explode
in *you* & begin again. Check-out time
is 11 AM & never comes early enough.

As at the casino, my steady loss of you
dribbled out its juice in unspent moments
each one thought to be second-to-last,

riding itself until the next bet. Highway
bridges are numbered helpfully in Kansas
as if to account for the bleeding but

not one of them sings a song by itself

Fried Potatoes and Alcohol
Marlys Cervantes

Oil sizzling in the skillet...
  never enough to eat with them,
Most months have at least a few days
  of living on only

fried potatoes and love
A bag of potatoes can go far when you're broke.
Love, well, we tried to

stretch it as far.
Friends coming to visit, to share the potatoes,
  could bring meat or vegetables,
    could bring diapers or formula,
But friends don't bring beef, or tomatoes, or onions, or baby needs
  when they visit.

Just alcohol.
No matter how little we had, that's what they'd bring
  even when you're broke,
    even when they're broke.

Home inked tattoos and cars running on fumes
Anger surfaces
  as each swallow slides
    down his throat,

destroying the lining that once was his stomach.
Little girls with skinned knees and dirty hands
  become big girls with broken hearts
    and sad smiles,
Bruises surround those tattered hearts
  and scar tissue envelopes them until

feeling cannot be found any longer.
Little boys who remember crying at the
  window when their mommies went out
    drinking, who grow up to be
Men who leave their wives and children to

drink.
Some days,
  potatoes and alcohol just don't lead to love

Oklahoma
W. L. Winter

In brave Minnesota there is a
line to the root, specific families,
shared ancestry, common heritage,

but I'm stuck here in this county,
my dreams scattered like seeds in
overgrown pasture, no deep tales
bind me, only the carvings of
our own new adventure and true
circles under the medicine wheel.

A tribe of orphans, bound by the blood
of shared years, work the harvest in the
field of hardship. The 49 and the ghost dance
bleed into the suburbs where casinos exact
revenge. We scratch the earth with iron
teeth to fill the coffer and the bowl.

The wind sometimes turns angry
and spins, but we joke at survival
and tease the quaking visitors
who cower under the long howl.

We know the darkness of loss
in our bones, that salt flavors
our biscuits like part of the recipe,
an ember in the campfire
that won't get stomped out,
we suck fire in our pipes and
drink the corn fermented.

Half Breed
W. L. Winter

I can't say why I loved them,
although I did. I never could
get close enough because of the
fences. Those young braves and I
blew off baseball for the same reasons.
Who needs that rack of rules when
long snakes of creeks will do?

Cut me in half and I turn the color
of olives, cut me lengthwise
and I bleed seeds into the wind.
It's a deep feeling, this in-between.

Downtown in the diner, I sense the
hidden order under their glassy smiles.
Drop the invisible ball and they will
turn on you, while the crude amongst
them hiss and strut like a banty rooster.

Take me to the frozen river and
stomp a hole with a wagon wheel,
then shove me into the current so
I can watch what's left of the sky
dancing up through the ice.

When I make it back to the flame,
that place where stories are told,
I'll take a smoldering twig and trace
a map in the sand, and if it suits me,
I'll point out that column of smoke
just over there on the horizon.

Report from the Outlying Territory
Lisa Lewis

tufts of animal fur sprigging barbed wire
something made it out alive

I wriggled through but my pants tore
I never was elegant slipping into small spaces

I balanced on two hard feet slicing raw pasture
I knelt to the scatter of ants

purpled balls of clover
various wars worming across deltas

photographs collected around the world
brown faces smeared in blood

white faces profiled beneath bright round helmets
the idea that they had already won

one slim body spearing the sky
olive on a toothpick except the sky is the olive

their story was not about getting stuck in Oklahoma
the story of sticking to a story

the story of the methane flare
its voice shaking

up there in the near sky short of clouds
when we say *take for granted* we are speaking of gifts

the small act of reaching for them as usual
as if we were picking flowers

puffing metallic air into ephemeral tires
drinking water to damp down an illness

I stripped off my jacket because the rain was stuck in the clouds
I stripped off my woolen shirt

lining my eyelids with a hot pencil
the better to peer into the split of the heavens

the soft place where the male god enters
I was planning to ride this one out

long I had claimed the right
to a taste for feathers

it was time to approach a friend at random
hand her something wrapped in paper

an award of sorts
I thought hard before I made my selection

filled her in on the particulars
the sun sagging into its sling

she studied the direction
she scratched long rays around a circle in the dirt

she used the longest stick she could find
I asked her if she knew where she was going

she had been sexed like a chicken
held to the light

she would only catch glimpses
careful little blades hacking the air

the toughest of the lilies coughing into its hands
she drew the saucepan

the short straw jabbed into quicksand
as if for breathing but nothing lives beneath

the story is we can forget about it
the story is nobody cares about that anymore

the methane flare trembling
because it heard we were coming for it

and the laws protect it like barbed wire
the laws bristle near it like plastic stars

or the new gun that anyone can own
and everyone does until it misfires

like striking a match in the part of your own hair
like breathing in the sharp, invisible carbon

Interstate Artery
Sly Alley

There is an Artery
that moves
my rabbit blood.
Transports it further
and farther
than a younger me
would have ever thought
possible.

October was the first time it moved me.
A couple years after the towers fell.
An Irish Car-bomb hangover in the
backseat. Headed to the Twin Cities.
My first time traveling through that state
named after my great-grandfather's
people.
Ioway.
Those corn fields that stretched

from horizon
to horizon.

And those years later
the Artery carried me south.
The land of the
Alamo.
Dried out creek beds
and dust devils
spiraling through
mesquite trees and
patches of peyote.
Riding back from Del Rio
with an Indian blanket.

For a while I lived in
Waxahachie.
They told me it was an

Indian word.

But I don't speak that tongue,
so I wouldn't know.
And anyway
the Artery didn't let me
stay there long enough
to find out for sure.

Blood moves.
For a while my blood
moved a lot.
These days it stays
near the heart.
But it's just a half hour drive
to hop on that Artery
and in a day
I can be back in
The Land of a Thousand Lakes
eating frybread, wild rice and venison

made by an Ojibwe man and his wife.
Or have a beer with Lakota George in
that old tavern in Northfield.

Or I can migrate south
to ride out a harsh Oklahoma winter
and have a taco with those
Kiowa boys
working the rail near Hondo.

Ancestors
Steve Sexton

I.
Ancestors speak through the wind.
I (try to) listen.
After all, the wind blows
in all directions.
I wonder how I might learn
the language of the wind,
wonder, that, if I do learn,
if their voices would become
a cacophony of ancient languages,
all of them yelling at me
to take my damn diabetes medication.

II.
You are no ancestor.
I know you too well.
You've been gone
twenty-six years this September.

I know you too well.
You are no ancestor.

Twenty-six years this September
you've been gone.

III.
The wind keeps blowing the cover off the expensive grill we bought
last summer. The grass is unkempt as it sways, almost violently. The
sky remains blue. Not like New Mexico, where the ancestors kick
up dirt, turning the vista brown, hazy, the sun struggling to break
through. One thing is obvious: The ancestors want me to grill tonight.

IV.
While loading the dishwasher,
scrubbing the tub,
dusting the living room,
sweeping, mopping the floor,
we have conversations.

The wind blows the red dirt,
collects on the dogs
as they shake, spreads
your voice throughout the house.
I sweep, scrub, gather, collect
each syllable, each word, each sentence,

each story,

pretend you are here,
holding the dust pan,
as I collect
deconstructed
memories.

V.
The Black Taoist poet
tells my class
that when the past appears,
do not engage it.
Simply let it be.
It will deconstruct itself.

I wonder how you will appear
after you've deconstructed
                              yourself.

I'm no Black Taoist poet.
I have trouble
not
engaging memories.

VI.
That time of the year
when it's too warm for the heater
too cold for the AC
so you open the windows the back door
let the voices blow
gently through the house

refreshing
restoring

VII.
The spring morning air is humid, oppressive.
Forecasters tell us
of the likelihood
of severe weather this afternoon
—tornados, strong ones.
Stay weather alert, aware of the vengeful wind today.

I imagine my ancestors
waking up on a morning
like this,
feeling the humid oppressive air,
looking at each other, saying,
"Shit's about to go down today."

VIII.
The Human GENOME project revealed
there is no race on a genetic level.
Our differences are physical, not genetic.

Race is a construct,
a madness we accepted.

I'm willing to live without race

because I know
when I bleed
it contains cells of my ancestors.

We construct race when we see the differences.
It might be soothing to you
to know you and I
are no different on a genetic level,
our madness is based on pigmentation.

But my eyes can't perceive the genetic level.

My blood may be constructed
by genetics
but my ancestors breathe
life

into those cells
into my pigmentation
into my constructs.

IX.
The grill cover the wind blows away,
that's sacred.
The dirt I sweep the dogs bring in,
that's sacred.
The styrofoam cup rolling down the street,
that's sacred.
My neighbor's tipped-over trash can,
wisps of hair constantly in my face,
high and low pressure systems
                    sweeping down the Plains,
that's sacred.

Deconstructed memories of you,
wisps of hair free from my ponytail,
pushing my car as I go down I-35,
the tornado siren,
sacred, sacred, sacred.

Council
J. D. Whitney

Five
    big
Oklahoma crows
sitting
      on the
ground
around
      one
red-tailed hawk.

The Great Run, Caldwell, Kansas, April 22, 1889
LeAnne Howe & Dean Rader

*50,000 people, European Immigrants reckless to claim Indige-
nous lands, parked along the borderline, waiting.*

I.

Forget Paris,
He said.
Free land,
He said.
Ours for the taking,
He said.
Crossing the line,
Mine.
Alle, alle, going,
Heading south to
Rivière rouge.

Forget Paris,
She said.
No public urinals,
No public putrefactions
No stinking Seine,
Land for *canards,*
She said.
Il ne faut pas cracher dessus,
It's not to be spit upon,
She said.
Giddyup,
C'est la vie.

Forget wild Indians,
50,000 Européens Settlers
Will not be stopped

She said.
One day we'll build
A route,
A road,
Carve a deep cut,
Right down the belly of the land,
A big I
Linking bistros, fruit stands,
Hat shops and fertilizer stores
Where now only weeds grow.
Giddyup,
C'est la vie.

II.

artery:

from the Latin artēria

+

the French *artere—*

meaning *trachea* or *windpipe*

believing, the Medievalists, to be a separate system than veins.

Arteries are bloodless after death
nothing, the ancient writers thought,

but air ducts.

In Greek, it is α [*aeirein* (to lift, to raise)],
from which Aristotle

created *aorte,*

which means "to hang" or more precisely,

that which is hung up

like [the thirty-eight Dakota

in Minnesota

terminus of the arterial highway system

of]
the heaving chest of this land—
trachea of trash &

truck tilt,
windpipe of washer water and waste—

aspiration at the great lake's
mouth.

III.

Forget Paris,
He said.
I want this to go on forever,
She said.
What?
Taking,
She said.
Of course,
He said.
Joyeuses Journées
Grasping,
Choking,
Clipping,
1,568 miles of skin
Off the land.

A big **I**
I can ride on,
Up and down,
Down and up,
She said.
To cut is not brutal,
We circumcise.

He gently buckles her on.
Giddyup,
C'est la vie.

IV.

Forget:

     and yet try to remember—

the body will always lay itself

     down, it will always find a way to stretch

into the into—

     beyond the borders of the self—

     both north & south

          up & down—
once,

the skin knew its land

the way a land knows history lost

to everything but itself—

once,

the land was its own

skin—

V.

Forget Paris,
She said.
Will settle Renfrow,
Dine on *Foie Gras* of The Moment,
Avec mustard seeds and wild onions.
Yes,
He said.
Will force feed ducks,
Making their livers grow 10 fold,
Cut small incisions on their necks so
They bleed to death.

Remember Renfrow,
Where we extract duck livers
With a sharp blade,
Lightly score both sides,
Sear in a red-hot dry skillet,
Sprinkle with coarse salt, pepper,
Swallow.
Voilà.

My Renfrow,
My Renfrow
She said.
A town born on the run,
Swelling beyond our wildest dreams,
120 in 1889.

Give me those wild open spaces
Without regulations,
He said.

Each morning,
Foie Gras with oranges and curry,
Noon,
Foie Gras with apples and chokecherries
And Night,
Foie Gras with green grapes and berries,
Before nighty-night,
Foie Gras with peanuts and prunes,
Forget Paris.
She said.
Follow the Big I-35
Linking sly horizons and miserly soils,
Linking waving wheat
That sure smells sweet,
With land's forgotten skin,
She said.
Giddyup,
C'est la vie.

VI.

Follow the big

              eye—

sly soil,
        miserly horizons—

towns born on the skin of regulations:

P
A
R
I
TULSA

an I on the run

[forget the small incisions on their necks]

qui n'avance pas, recule

[remember the sharp blade]

m I n n e s o t a

somewhere,
        off in the distance

a girl rides her horse
        across the Atlantic ocean

maneuvers her Motobécane
        from Dallas to Duluth—

    land never gets what it needs

        or what it deserves.

    Where is land yours?

        Where do you bury to be wanted?

What skin is your color?

frontier:

from the French *frontier,*

    meaning the front line of an army—hence

                to attack, resistance *[faire frontière]*—
        it means, the front
                    line.

Tall Grass Prairie

In My Original Kansas, When We Were Iron
Jennifer Boyden

First there was how my brain
was blanked by the depression.
Drinking to bring the brain back
makes you wake up
forgetting how to read. I forgot
the word for face, forgot
how to turn napkins
into animals and if
the stars still made silver.

Thank you for asking,
but before I could write
to tell you how I'm doing,
I had to learn to drive past
neon lights and liquor stores
and to stand upright at parties
without putting my hands
down people's pants or asking
if the corner near the clustered plants
was a good place for crying.

I came back and remembered
words that lived in my original Kansas.

The Kansas we knew 500 years ago
when we were a wagon wheel
and a stick-dragged line—
and the Kansas of all the years before that,
from the Big Bang through to protozoa
and right up to the moment
of having arms and air freshener
so when we sell our houses
it smells like we learned to cook.

I came back and am learning
to make pizza from a box.
I am ordering boxes

and am grateful for how much they do.
They produce food and clothing
and build towers in the garage.
They are how we get so many things
into our houses: boxes arrive on the porch
and inside of them is a whole life
you can just switch on with a remote
or hang from walls or eat. Hams
and snack cakes. Harmonicas.
Buckets for throwing up.
I am learning kale. I am learning soup
and how to make it
without using a can
opener as the stirring spoon.
I am learning that an empty box
is the daughter's magic castle
whose wish is that you will remember
how not to sleep.

After the long depression
I had three selves:
the one who can still feel
the ungraspable edges and the sliding down,
the one who believed it was over
and so threw flowers at the sun,
and the one who saw those first two
selves from the great distance
and felt the tenderness
of inevitability: I would happen
to myself again
and I would happen to myself
again, and this meant
goodbye, goodbye, goodbye.

This meant ants on the meat tray.
This meant friends
who write to ask where I am.
How should I know?

I am in three places.
We are all crossing the street together:
the first self afraid to be hit by the car,
the second just happy
to know the word for street
because it is enough some days
to have a single word.
And the third who understands
both that the car will hurt
and that the street is a long way away
because I am also a sky. I am a sky

the same way I am Kansas: a body
of dust, a body of evaporate and dissipate
and windblown brick.
Kansas in my dog blood.
Kansas before it was named.

I arrived there because it was already in me.
Little Kansas, it said, and I arrived
into myself and into the good red dirt,
the good brown dirt, the dirt of departures
blown in from the far side
of the country, passing through, settling,
and moving on.

Little Kansas, you are dragging a stick
to find your way back,
but the wind says no.
The trail you scraped
showing the way back is blown over
so now your arrival is everywhere.
The dirt of my self / Dirt of where to plant next.

Thank you for asking how I am doing.
It hadn't occurred to me
that the question could feel so active:
the *doing* part.
I am putting books in boxes.
I am packing up my daughter's room.

I am asking the spoons not to multiply.
I am separating light from dark
as if morning is not a season.
Doctors agree that mornings
are the most difficult.
That's when the lying begins
about how the day will go, a day
when I remain fully dressed and upright
among pine trees or people with nothing
but gorgeous coffee in that cup.
This is all before a bird hits the window
and the whole plan unravels
and then you have to apologize
to the plates for throwing them.
They shouldn't have to break like that.
No one should break like that.

Sometimes I am grateful for my vanity.
I used to hate it: the way I ran
from one shadow to the next
so the sun wouldn't fill my skin
with Kansas. But then I read
how drinking and weeping sags
the jowls and bursts the veins
and that was another reason
to quit. Now I smile
even while reading the terrible news
because I need to make smile lines.
If there is still beauty available,
I want to give it a chance, make
a path for it to come in on.
Dear Beauty: you have a week
to arrive. After that, all promises
are radio static, they're snow in May.

After that, I may fall in love again
with my sheets. They are the hotel
of my dreams.
There, my drowning self can miss
entire life cycles of frogs.

My singing self would like to see them hatch.
And the faraway self understands
the frogs will emerge again
and then again, each year
until one of those other selves
has won. The winning self will declare
which one I finally am:
The Sleeper, The Singer?
I may become the one who rises
for polliwogs and hears
flagellate pulsings encoded by star-speak.
No, I may sleep in tadpole darkness
and miss their forthcoming selves. Perhaps
I will be the one who makes small hats
for each of them and calls them
by their first name: Home.
Thank you for asking.

I have been to Kansas my whole evolutionary history.
I have been a sky and a bed,
and they are not that different.

In Kansas, the earth is blown into bricks
and stacked until summer is an oven.

It is where animals come in trucks.
It is permitted to boil animals in Kansas, to clarify
their blood and sell it
in bricks for soup and for the heart,
which desires to be coursed through
by blood.

I also should ask how you are doing
except I can't recall
what we shared between us.
It was a wet sheet in August,
a haircut in September.
I entered Kansas
before there was lice on earth,
and stayed until the lice were complete,
eventually picked out by hands
that dot-to-dotted me

back together, calling me daughter daughter,
sister sister, mother mother.
When they talk to you like that,
it is hard to say no
to waking up. In this world.
In this world. Where the food
can't grow itself.
Where your elders are asking
where they're from. Where the concrete
is as close as the city kids will ever get
to a mountain: Mount Incremental Loss.
Mount Wagonload of Mountain
Until the Mountain is Gone.

You can be many things
if you listen to where your blood
has lived before it became so personal:
so person bound. Before that,
had you been the rain much?
Had you answered ink
with a wobbling song?
Does iron remind you of any blood you know?
Do you remember how to let go
of your feathers?
It's a muscle release, the letting go,
so the body can escape
into the underbrush.
Your rising sap self,
your microscopic cellular self.

You were so small before blood
found a way into you,
but you were always on the way.

I remember we shared some iron.

It was when our meteor selves
traveled to get here. We had to slam
into earth to make this life happen,
the constellations at our backs.

The world made shapes
out of oncoming you
and reshaped them right up until you,
and will go on shaping after. Remember

when we arrived in Kansas
on our own hooves,
meat heavy and reading the grass
that was printed on the air.
Water was a cluster place
and we found it with our flat-toothed mouths,
our muzzle-soft faces. We looked at the stars
and divided. I was nickel. I was heave.
I was iron red and an ocean full of shapes
who still remember us.

We looked at the stars
and made more of them
from our ungulate lowing.
We were on the way to now.
The glaciers dropped their stones
and called it sleep. Thanks for asking

how I am doing. I am not sure
that today will be the kind of day
where the road works.
I'm not sure it's straight enough
to get us to the next city
full of my boxes. When I lived
in Kansas, it was redundant: just what happened
because I couldn't remember
my blood had been there already.
It called me back and I went
because I couldn't remember
I'd been there since the beginning.
When you don't remember
your original Kansas nothing goes
right. Paul drank everything
and almost died and Tony ate steak
on Valentine's Day because nothing
except meat sent him notes
written in red, and Carl just kept

getting married.
Were we the slowest cluster ever?
Stars that divided and divided
or got sucked back into themselves
and went cold?
Time led up to now, when we made
a world where cows could arrive by truck
so we could eat them faster
and not have to see their star eyes,
their I-was-you-once faces.
In Kansas, they process the animals
and it smelled like scorched coffee
until I saw the processing floor and then
it smelled like memory loss.

Once on the cutting floor
I saw a long red braid
in the corner mixed with blood.
I wanted to know—I still want to know—
if whoever had worn that braid
cut it to get away from that room
or just ran out of things to cut. And so cut.

Who leaves such a history
to the scouring hose?
How long could I last on top of this blowing earth.

Thank you for asking. Sometimes
I am nowhere and sometimes
I become a place.

What of trucking in the animals
to cluster them to our hunger?
They ask for water at the slaughterhouse,
and no one answers them with water.
Before all the Kansas growing in us,
we could have been water.
Our hunger could have been their cluster place.
We could have gone to them. It is easy
to be water. It's like downhill.
It's like sugar.

You looked
like stars as you divided and divided.
They call you brother brother.
If you can't hear them, ask your blood
who will answer them with iron.
I appreciate that you asked, because
it means I am still here.
I could not always say that.
Not when I was gone, just before
I became the three selves. You will wonder
what opened up to let those selves through.

That's what I'm telling you.
It's the first Kansas. It drew me
to it and let me go. Come back,
it said, and I came back.
Go now, it said, and I left
but could not find my way.
Draw your cells as circles, it said,
and I did.
Follow their magnetic pull, it said,
and I went west until I had a baby
who drew circles and crossed all
the circles out and my husband feared
that they were eyes
and tried to wake me up.
He knew me when we were sand.

When I asked him if we'd hit Kansas yet,
he said we had never left. It is all the same.

When they handed us water we bloomed
and I feared the bloom.
I went into water and understood
I was water already. I drank it
because I know how to drink
whatever is near and in my hand.
I drank the water and water
and water until I
always had water in my hand
and nothing else, until I became

the cluster place of my own gathering
and the cluster place of star blood.

And when my daughter asked
if I was now able to walk
with her to the top of a hill
for the first day of spring,
I said yes because I knew how
to get there, and because I knew
the long way down.

Assembly of God
J. D. Whitney

Check all parts
against
enclosed list.

Follow
directions
carefully.

Kansas Wind:

J. D. Whitney

"First time
I seen
     my
dog
     blow
over
peein'
     on
3 legs."

Riding a Low Ridge in Southern Kansas
Doc Arnett

On the first Sunday in June,
the sort of mild but sunny day
that sometimes comes soon after May,
I rode toward the river
on Geuda Springs Road just north of Ark City.

The smell of ripening wheat
sifted through a slight eastern breeze
as I turned toward Udall and pedaled up the long slope.

Old free-form posts splotched with lichen
and stapled with heavy-rusted strands of wire
strung along the bank,
wavy forms that shouldered the edge of the field,
defining the boundary between
the fine-drilled lines of hope that men intended
and what happens to grow beside the road.

Off to the west,
along the suede-vested bottoms of the Arkansas River,
long blades of shoulder-high corn shimmered in the sun,
sweeping seams of silver and green glimmering soft reflections.

An abrupt rise of hardwoods ran in straight lines
along the fences, intersecting corners
and twisting along the ditches and streams
that drain into the sand-strained channel.

Miles beyond that,
an hour's ride from here,
the great spokes of turbines mined the wind
in their slow spin,
sending a collective surge through black wires
spired between tall spines of creosoted pine,
rising above asphalt and grass,
above rank weeds and the seeds of grain,
above everything but the tallest cottonwoods

gentling rustling the shadows of leaves
across the face of quiet waters
passing beneath an old bridge
where swarms of swallows have lived
for as long as anyone can remember.

I could ride for days
in a thousand different places
and see nothing finer than this.

After the Grass Fires
Benjamin Myers

My friend Phil, the shuffle-step macabre,
pulls his oxygen tank behind

him on a hand truck. White dogs
come back from sooty fields

a grimmer shade of bone. Phil is thin
in snake-skin boots & walks to the Maverick-mart

for beer (also on the hand truck). Most days
he paints—Mick Jagger in drag, Rocky

& Bullwinkle on roller skates—& eats
dry cereal for dinner again. We watch

the news at 10:00: they show
the interview with a rancher & his son,

how they stood up to their chins
in the dirty farm pond, holding down

the horse while flames scribbled
darkly in the margins. Another word

for *human* is brown paper and twine.
Yesterday the scrub oak & red cedar

burned like the heart of a saint & the flame-
cleared fields revealed lost tools, arrow heads,

animal bones. Another word for *human*
is—I forget. There is a cement slab

in the burned grass, a bathtub, toilet
& sink in open sunshine. Across

the slab a chimney reaches
like a one armed man for God. Oh yes,

the word is *tinder*.

What to Do after a Tornado
Benjamin Myers

Tell them it sounded like a freight train—
they like that—
even if it sounded like your stepfather
taking off his belt, even if it sounded
like the crying baby born in the gym
bathroom during prom. Tell them you never

saw it coming, even if that black wind
had been turning just over your shoulder
since sixth grade. Then excuse yourself

to gather photos scattered through the rubble,
but don't pick up your own. There
are happier families. Look for one of a girl

in blue shorts, aged ten, standing
beside a Ferris wheel with a pink storm cloud
of cotton candy hovering over one hand.
She will be you.

Watch the crows pick through piles
of broken sheetrock and wet carpet.
Throw them what's left of your lucky deck of cards.

When the newspaper man asks you to pose
beside the lone standing closet
where you hid beneath winter coats
and Christmas decorations,
try not to smile for the camera: no one
else should know that you are about
to walk clearly, cleanly, completely
away.

keep my ghosts
MW Rishell

they keep my ghosts where they belong there were places I dared
not tread I didn't go North and I didn't go West as those were roots
everywhere they are at closed Joyland which has no more joy at
Twin Lakes and at Towne East they are my favorite Mexican joint on
Broadway and Church's Chicken near campus my ghosts are at Kirby's
still fighting fights of the mind long ago and my homes my bars ceased

a long time ago The Flicker The Grape The Cedar I left for
thirty years on my own rail behind new places where warehouses
glowered where bums would gather cheap champagne near the tracks
the big press printed the trendiest galleries and other gems discov-
ered rediscovered and reimagined those jewels make my city shine it is
not my city though I am still my city but my ghosts keep drinking

Little Kings with classmates in the foundations of homes in the
neighborhood I now live of a time when I knew how to dodge trains
stalled keeping me on my side of town the sides of country roads
near tilled fields where I made out with high school girlfriends
thirty years later they live in those same spots in homes graced to send
their children to suburban schools not a part of me I know my city

those aren't my people their green grass keep my ghosts at home
fighting keeping the white flight mowing their sharply edged lawns

A Cover and a Lie
MW Rishell

States' Rights is a lie and
The Cost of Doing Business is a cover

A man won't raise the cost of his product
His desperate staff are in the kitchen graying
While their children are in the streets playing
In the wallet, Mom and Dad are getting fucked

States' Rights is a lie and
The Cost of Doing Business is a cover

A man in Topeka indicted for misconduct
Can't see that evil is his byproduct
From the House they can't see spirits breaking
It's their own people they're forsaking

State's Rights is a lie and
The Cost of Doing Business is a cover

The chicken in every pot is getting plucked
As the politicians work to obstruct
A drive-by brings a new slaying
At work Junior's parents are praying
Basic human rights seem defunct

States' Rights is a lie and
The Cost of Doing Business is a cover

The Flesh of Hands
J.B. Hutchens

As a child I knelt in streams
cupping water in my hands
seeing how long I could hold it.
However tight I pressed
the water seeped through
unseen cracks and creases
between my fingers that
I could never understand.
Now I know flesh is imperfect,
especially the flesh of hands.

As a child I cupped
my grandfather's hands in mine
seeing how long I could hold them.
However tight I pressed
he slipped through
unseen cracks and creases of eternity
that I will never understand.
Now I know that the flesh of hands
have labored long days.

As a man I do not try to cup
anything too tight in my hands
prejudiced as I am by childhood.
I only watch the cracks and creases
in the flesh of my hands
grow wider and deeper as years pass.
Now at the stream I no longer worry
about holding onto anything.
I only run my hands through the water,
and the water passes by.

Jubilate: Burden, Kansas
Siobhán Scarry

For grain dust is fine and slips through the fingers.
For grain becomes bread that we break in your memory.
For grain is transported by ships and trains and long flat boats.
For grain is stored in buildings that rise up from flat land.
For grain elevators are strangely the poetry of the American sky.
For they are built in various shapes according to landscape and
    function.
For the buildings are pure in their geometry.
For the circle is unity.
For the triangle is the trinity.
For square and rectangle are pleasing in their shapes.
For the hexagon is the geometry of the bee.
For bees, in their building of honeycombs, gave rise to the
    schematics of interlocking grain bins.
For hexagonal bin design does not waste space—there is no need
    for the strangely shaped interstitial bins.
For the longest elevator in the world uses hexagonal bin design—
    Praise the grain elevator in Hutchinson, Kansas.
For elevators are made of many materials.
For we are woken to life by knowing decay.
For wood is decay.
For tile decays.
For steel bins do not insulate the grain.
For vermin get inside the bins and gorge themselves on the fine
    dust of harvest.
For life is decay.
For the abandoned silos are in decay.
For there is dust in our lungs.
For all creatures will come to dust.
For it is true—and I have seen it—that grain dust explodes.
For spontaneous combustion is proof of a Presence—Remember
    the thirty-three men who died at the Husted Mill in 1913.
For dust clings to elevators, even those converted to hotels and
    artists' lofts.
For firstly, the grain is moved upward in the elevator by small
    buckets on conveyor belts.
For secondly, the grain is moved to the distributing floor, where it
    is weighed and chalkboards mark the weight and grade and

destination.

For thirdly, the grain is moved along conveyor belts and lowered into the bins through small holes that the men try not to fall through.

For fourthly, the grain is stored for months or years or else it is moved quickly through chutes onto boats or railcars waiting below.

For the storage and transport of grain is a wholesome enterprise.

For it is pleasing to feel the slip of grain between the fingers and hear it crunch underneath boots on the cement workfloor—Be gracious to the elevator in Burden, Kansas.

For each handful of grain comes from a field of growing things—Be gracious to the cribbed wooden elevator in Attica, Kansas.

For fields from above are geometrically pleasing—Save the condemned silos of Minnesota.

For there is Presence in the swish and movement of grain particles colliding in the chutes.

For the storing of grain in large bins is the desire for tomorrow—Bless the peeling letters of *C* and *T* and *A* on the silo in Lake City, South Dakota.

For the Dakotas are desolate and need their landmarks.

For those states have been spared with silos spaced evenly along the railroad, every fifteen miles.

For people in Kansas are more needy—Bless the four-mile intervals.

For there is something to be said for the even spacing of certain kinds of structures.

For it is important to love the spaces in between—Remember the interstitial bins with shapes that accommodate.

For flat-bottomed bins are useless for unloading but have pleasing shapes.

For flat land must have shapes that rise up in praise. Bless Aldo Rossi.

For silos desire upward motion.

For the workfloor is the ground level—Praise the wooden elevator of Chokio, Minnesota.

For the storage bins are the body of the building—Give us this day our daily bread.

For the distributing floor has many windows but workers keep their eyes on the floor to avoid falling through—Praise the buckling slats of the elevator in Lucas, Kansas.

For the headhouse sits on top of the building—Bless the small dusty windows of elevator headhouses.

For any structure so solid is a monument to the everlasting—A blessing on Danville, Kansas, where the eighteen-bin silo dwarfs the church (bless its steeple and the lonely slatted window).

For structures this large have SPIRIT inside them.

For SPIRIT is fullness.

For SPIRIT is round in its shape.

For round structures have no end and converge with the sky in an understanding of infinity.

For it is most common for grain bins to be round.

For common shapes are pleasing to the gods.

For storage is proof of thinking of tomorrow.

For allow me to consider a single spark in Wichita, Kansas.

For every spark does not ignite.

For desire cannot be predicted.

For sparks are in every careless cigarette lit on the workfloor.

For sparks fly from the steel rails of nearby train tracks.

For fire is the particular fear of grain elevator workers.

For fire CONSUMES.

For CONSUME is a word that feeds on itself, desires more than itself.

For the word keeps circling in the mouth when you are done saying it.

For a spark with the desire to CONSUME felled the DeBruce grain elevator four miles southwest of Wichita, Kansas.

For due to management negligence, on June 8th, 1998, a concen—trator roller bearing seized from no lubrication and locked the roller into a static position as the conveyor belt continued to roll over it.

For this is called the "razor strop" effect—Imagine machinery at 260 degrees Celsius.

For these are the conditions that join fire with dust.

For seven men died that day for America's bread—Rest the souls of Jose Luis Duarte (41 years), Howard Goin (64 years), Lanny Owen (43 years), Victor Manuel Castaneda (26 years), Raymundo Diaz-Vela (23 years), Jose Prajedes Ortiz (24 years), and Noel Najera (25 years).

For even in its hell-bent desire, the spark could not reach all the bins.

For steel is strength.

For concrete is strength.
For the metal clasps on the lunch boxes are strength.
For the flat land is filled with structures that are still standing.
For when traveling in certain states, one elevator passes from view
    just as another appears on the horizon.
For elevators carry the eye upward to sky.
For elevators reach.

Old 81

Siobhán Scarry

Up from the shorn fields in insect waves, this undulating migration of small black birds,
ribbon raveling free of any machinery of longing that might fasten—

     Fieldlift. Foxed culverts.
             Pre-stressed concrete company in its morning ablutions: idling, idling

I plucked myself out like an oculus

tore at the roots, left the searching feelers to desiccate in the scorch and shine

We wake and water, snack and hairbrush, shape hands into shoehorn, then travel the road to
Hesston—plumb line into the hot heart of the country

     Milo. Wheat. Soybean.
             Etched longitude of 1855: Sixth Principal Meridian of the U.S.

Surveyors set the staff and compass here for fear of "Indian trouble" further west—reason
for the road as vexed as our nation's reasons for being

     Hold us all
             responsible for the enormity of our decisions

Why must hands ever take that shape?

     Reed break. Scissored apostrophe. Shudder-crouch.
             And we add our names to these fields of living things

See Fig. 1: a body torqued through necessity's engines into an arc, to harbor your
small body & my own, amniotic world in the world until in rushes all the rest,
without shelterbreak of these first and foremost—

Plastic bags snagged and ghost-fluttering in the long lines of hedge, singing of the wind

Signage that makes an error of possession: THE CHURCH OF CHRIST WELCOME'S YOU

How the errant apostrophe in "welcome" digs at the mindcalm of morning & birds & broken
balers & boxcars boxcars oiltankers ad infinitum neighbor us on the path to preschool drop-off

A first philosophy: nipple-latch and snack pack, wielding, working, worlding with love & every fiber fashioned into the protean shapes care will take, this thin bright stretch of Kansas

Liniment. Landscape. Poultice. Price.
　　(for so long I could not rend or render the self toward anything futural)

Old 81, Meridian Highway, rural two-lane, no rumble strips at midline or shoulder, road forcing the instincts forward, tight to the wheel, return to first feeling, self-preservation—

This law I learned to love again (major mover)
　　　　my mouth, this clotted shape of sound, the only way I know

to come back to the error of apostrophe, daily roadside call to prayer at the altar of inevitable misstep, each day I soften to the fact of errancy, move closer to forgiveness of my own—

Haircut & shoeshop. Nightterror. Gardengrow.

The line of starlings lift and breathe toward the blank page of sky, and from the backseat, reverent of all that is new, you tell me *mama, I can't see where it ends*

Weather
Patricia L. Meek

I.
There is weather,
so says my mother to my father.
She means to say, *a storm is blowing through.*
He laughs because he knows that
it is true. There is always weather.

II.
I hiked to the slot canyon today
with someone else, not you.
But you managed to tag along—
an invisible form—a child draped over
me—a presence that never really goes away.

You are a fondness that promises to be filled
by the physical
as the shoehorn of this day's light
slides into the heel of dusk.
Everyone else gets to commute home
to be with someone they adore and despise.

Without your body attached to your affection,
technically, you are not here.
Someone else needs to tell this to the deep knowing of my heart.
It won't hear me when I say, she's gone.
I'm tired of talking.

III.
You must have silently practiced the word *break*
in your thoughts for weeks.
After your return from the cabin, your truth was solidified like
a desert rock. I kept repeating—*are you sure?*—
hoping to crack you open.

I left in such a hurry that there remained
on the plate in the sink
my teeth marks in the soft heel of bread.
Who knew it was our last meal?

IV.
You have become a type of barometric pressure,
the subtlest form of weather. The most painful
for one who has become blind and must rely on other senses.
You leave behind sensations of *being*—
like a ghost.

Sometimes I feel your regret,
but it is not enough to bring you home.

V.
The woman who is not you points out the
dusty indentations of what passed as rain in the night.
It looks like the markings of a fossil.

We crunch along the trail, descending toward irrigation.
The dogs have scattered out in the direction of cows.
I feel the high desert's desperation.
In this drought, colors have faded.
I can feel you on my skin. You are still very much alive.

VI.
Water echoes against the red canyon rock,
no less a miracle than the lives we become.
I sometimes forget how fragile it all is.

The woman not you sits down beside me on a black rock.
She takes in a full breath, marvels at how surreal this is.

Just like Alice in Wonderland.

Down the rabbit hole, I look up at the
vast, oceanic sky. I look for traces of your stormy eyes.
What I see is the lazy form of clouds, collecting, building.

All life has such urgency when there is lack.
It is not easy to hold space for the dying—so
I want to believe like children do
in the power of my will.

I will this to be the monsoon.
I will that the love I feel from you be in a form that I can touch once more. And that love is enough to keep clouds tracking together long enough to sustain life.

I do not want to believe that—more often than not— thunderheads simply break apart.
I do not want to believe that when I return from my Odyssey, you will not be home.

The Intrinsic Essence of Hay

Roy Beckemeyer

"... the cows ... caring nothing for all this,
Their noses in incense hay... "
- Robert Bly, "A Walk"

Sun-warmed scent of hay rolls in fields,
the moist center still on its way
to drying: alfalfa, brome, bluestem,
switchgrass, lespedeza. The cows
sniff, lift their heads a bit, compare
notes on aromas: protein stewing
in the bright day, cut stems still
oozing sweet plant sap, green chlorophyll
turning amber, then gold. Their rumens
rumble; their stomachs run riot.

Sandhill Seasons
Roy Beckemeyer

Spring: Courtly Dancers

Sandhill cranes would never deign to dance
to Britten's piece from *Gloriana*
however glorious they might consider spring,
however much they might resemble
Renaissance dandies in tights and trunkhose,
for they dance wings-akimbo, more akin
to jesters than knights, bound up
out of fields of grass, call their own rhythm,
bend and bow, skinny legs incongruous
beneath the mass of body, awkward hops
giving no insight into how they will soon
waltz away into the wilderness of sky.

Autumn: September Sonata

As September leans into October
cranes mount the air, watch the world
take on a Technicolor cast as they go.
Their calls more chortle than challenge,
their aims avocational now, no longer
charged with the urgency of spring.
They jaunt southward, jigging, jagged lines
of birds, legs trailing, necks leading,
and those wings, that take up so much
of the sky, wave to the awestruck world
as they fly.

Horizons

Roy Beckemeyer

"Back toward the time when
the world, without footprints, broke open"
—Ginger Murchison, from her poem,
"On Stone Mountain"

A backhoe paws its single front
      leg onto gray shale, shatters, pulls
breaks, delaminates, lays waste

the traces of *Edaphosaurus*
      dog-paddling hot, briny estuaries
under equatorial Permian sun,

rips pages of ancient stone
      texts, devastates cuneiform
signatures of reptilian claws,

the clay tablets of milennia
      of evolution's accounts, the world,
with footprints, broken open.

Wintering Prairie
Megan Kaminski

Snow drifts the prairie white
each gathering a prayer a knife a candle
water crystalline seeding warmth
ground expectant bootfall above sod
the ground between ground we share
ground that sprouts green holds roots deep
soft porous mealy with bug and vole
and this poem will be a long one
will widen will drift snow
language like dribbles and arctic chill
will stretch to Dakota fox alone in the field
to field mice buried deep
will follow the compass's pull magnetic north
oil in shale beneath us tallgrass roots beneath us
bodies of fathers and mothers beneath
us the sod the Kanza-call warmth of snow on this
day will stretch north to you and children by the fire
to pipelines and trains and fractures in bedrock
arctic-alpine fingernail clam and mourning cloak
will carry me warranted in sound breath encased

I do not cry
I do not tarry
I do not break
on this cold day

Long shadows and sun-melt spread
across lawns across asphalt
neighborhood strip mall and shop
spread west past town into farm
past county line and field
cottonwoods on the river
switch grass and bluestem crowd
over limestone around barbed fence
tree-creak warm goat-graze in sunned patches
this afternoon this house-break this reprieve
from bone-chill and ache this call this flutter
dry leaf on a branch light coating shadow
this grasping for mile after mile
this swallow this sigh this heartcrush
hair bone skin made tissue from
dirt from water from sun from mineral
temper this break and empty balance
tally our remaining days

Morning toll campanile echo
through the valley over the frozen lake
graying sky barely gray more
an absence a want for things
to come that will not green trash receptacle
green hose evergreen bush
hardly green tipped in snow
the widest main street in Plains, Kansas,
twenty cars deep median treed and empty
wheel tred wind wobble call and kaw
no people just wind down today's street
no plows scraping asphalt concrete
no boot-tracks through field
hawk-call and chimney-smoke

Muddy boots inside the door
bricked salt-brined
another day started the same pallor
hour indistinguishable from hour
water-logged field brown grass brown
twig on ground on branch
mini-van grayed from the week
and quiet this intersession
lull between holiday and heavy
drag of ice down cocked roof
cold-carry of virus and spore
lungs wrenched open dry sputter
birds flocked out the window
cedar-berries warmed to taste
slow migration north snow receding
pit and berry seed and spittle
expectation of months far-flung

And in absence no flowering
old snow piled corner high in parking lots
these same bare branches and wind howl
clouds wall up the western sky snow flurry
and tire screech contrails fading east
murmurs from north ghost this morning
my heart-swallow my back-fade
lines carry from forehead to page to prairie
disintegrating town and county
marsh memory of coot and woodcock
gar and spadefoot and ringneck snake
black shadow across lawn dry leaf glimmer
this memory this place this warble-cry

I carry absence
I carry want
I carry body ache
on this bright day

Motherless this morning
dry wind and daybreak slow
white tatters cast cloud
on ground on browned grass on bodies
layered permeable
layered tissue softening
squirrel-hop and leaf-shiver
response to questions unearned
no answer no sigh
parcels pack into truck beds
ice melt in gutters
skin cells slough off
dust the field our faces
giving way making room
absorptive clay and limestone
wet-rot and daily decay

Snow drifted to knee
front barricade of white
warm seep turned ice
a ridge a remainder
a crescent opening north
eyes malnourished too bright
to bring leaf or tree
or handprint into focus
field-follow and scatter
ice pellets across the ground
across town and holding syllables
gathering us close yielding
day to shadow to owl-call

A Darker Land
A.H. Hofer

is most desired, fertile, blessed,
fed by the blood and drool of murder, the hunt,
the collapsed diseased and the old, their
                            untold
horizons of mineral and mold, layered
worm-loved skin and bone.

It has been the way
of all heartland since each first step's evolution.

Otherwise,
what good could it be, a wedding dress in a box,
sustenance for a moth or two, a mouse house
curiosity for reptilian swallowers of pain -
certainly no land for lilacs, however forlorn
for their brevity, nor verdant bean,
nor corn—
            a sand, only, and only venom
becoming born.

Pages must turn and burn for a right birth,
must burn into little black rose leaves,
their messages disperse like dry-rotted veils
opened to the wind -
                  so let fall all the villages,
torch the crack-stick forests, human, beast
and tool.

For the blackest grounds
                  birth
the sweetest wheats; what feeds on such
muscles to the most flavorful meats.

Any mother knows.

An infant suckles milk from the breast,
nourishment our first need of the dead, though
never in a place where the rich dust

can't dance its orbed delight,
sunbeam spotlight or no.
                              The motes are numbered,
the number the price, though the calculations
of natural math no human may figure.

The mother coos, the skin sheds the days.

A darker land,
ancient mathematician
and a god of the feed, has no trouble
keeping count of its needs.

Weep Willow
Denise Low

Whip-snap willows plié arcs
most like water's ripples,
"In slow relief, / their incredible /
years-long ballet,"

Peeled inner bark, shining wet,
hoops held I lace tight.
"Lithe at first, / until they bow
/—absolute—."

Saplings tangle fishlines,
cottonwood roots, muskrat holes:
"no leaf has fallen nor / bitten by the sun
/ turned orange or crimson."

Silver leaves minnow currents
—long teardrops, drowning.
"The leaves cling and grow paler,
/ swing and grow paler."

Veil of flutter branches,
bead-strand doorway:
"It is a willow when summer is over,
/ a willow by the river."

"Every one/has to learn
/ humility."
I grieve the willow washed
away a friend gone.

Bank collapses. Bole leans over
water too far undercut,
"oblivious to winter, / the last to let
go and fall."

Water Monster weirs,
wood unmoored, twisted,
"floods take them—/ They have to swim,
/a few stragglers / to a bend."

Note: "Weep Willow" uses lines from William Stafford's poem "Willows" (used with permission) and William Carolos Williams's "Willow Poem" (public domain).

Stomp Dance, Wyandotte County
Denise Low

The lead man lifts his black hat and calls from the center.

I wait for the tail end of the man-woman procession. Lead women are shell shakers. Double-time steps rustle turtle shell rattles tied to shins.

Men sing and sing loud. Women step-step hard. The inner circle might turn to the fire and dance sideways.

My grandfather and grandmother lived on Lenape Delaware land near this spot. Their footprints remain in this ground.

The leader raises his arm for each new song. Men answer him. Their breath lifts into smoke and wind.

I remember *Jo sa yi*, what he said about tobacco. The head man offers it to fire.

I remember the Fall Leaf family and their stomp ground near Copan. I remember Cherokees who dance, Redbird Smith's descendants Croslin and Benny.

Some songs are older than Kituwah Mound. Tunes and rhythms resound.

She-shush she-shush mixes with whistles of night hawks. Dance is a night-long prayer.

Chicory Afternoon
Denise Low

Sky-snatched galaxies burst.

      Porcupine is a nimble fat man's shadow.

Greens are seven calories a plateful:
add sugar and vinegar.

      Fireplace sun flattens earth edges.

Like bachelor buttons, midday blue, cornflowers—
these weedy stems travel ditches.

      A single Doric column stands in grass,
      broken bird bath, basin vanished.

Roadside asphalt cracks into *raku*,
      fills with budded stems.

      Lifeless brown-crested flycatcher—
      red-satin piping, yellow-brushed—
      lies gravel-graved.

Not coffee but
steep the dark root musk.

It Is All Just a Line on a Page
Jim McCrary

The original three-five was
Of course
The Mississippi running
As it still does
Pretty much from Canada to
The Gulf of Mexico and beyond
Sitting in an outdoor café in Veracruz, Mexico
One can, should one, I imagine, feel the
Mississippi push from up in Louisiana.

Living just a bit west of 35
Lawrence is a one day walk from KC
If you're on either the Oregon or Santa Fe or California
Trail… as it was then as now.

Again that vertical swath called Thirty-Five
Still raises enough dust to make it visible
To some
The "inside passage" so to speak

The crossing, as it is visible
Becomes the I Seven Zero
Which splits the country horizontal

And with the I-Ninety just a bit north
Creates an equal sign across this
The midsection. Should one wish
To relocate to Denver or perhaps Cheyenne.

Drovers who left Kansas City had
Choices and one either chooses to follow
Or not…your choice.

The trails, still visible in the deep ruts of wheels
Which one can walk out too from here
In Lawrence
Should one choose too

South west, South south west, west, west north west.
Oregon, Butternut, Santa Fe, California,
Splitting the country

As today the I-Three Five
Just another way to get
From here to here again

What's left behind lies
Alongside where we are

Sea of Grass
Joe Harrington

Westerly my love approaches me
Love is a word she could
Tire in the open sun
We fill up with clouds above the sky
The universe is turning up there
Brings a huge terrain of soapstone tarrying
Finally binding in the sense of
No one will know about our love
When those who remember us die
We thing or think of our love as pastoral
Not brief lunches between car trips
Trips up ideas of easiness, like
Wrestling, not dancing, too much
Shattering talking remember when
We remembered
Anytime we meet we smile eventu-
Ally even on our odd days, long,
Years, short
A tailored system scissors a punky
Sunset, a set of stylized hearts,
Circular moving incarnate storm
Within our small time, the tides
Going back and forth, winds
Blow mostly westerly

In William S. Burroughs' Yard
Joe Harrington

bare back

      bunny

            froze

did not

      "make" it

    murky snowmelt

minor

      chilly henbit

              "cosas de la vida"

frostbit

      tulips

          blasted

but yonder—

           a live rabbit—

                    good luck!

The Central Hiway
Joe Harrington

fluorescent orange
interloper
nibbles generic

grape jelly as
sun breaks   an
oriole

blackpoll warblers bottled
up in the park
north wind   head wind

the poem an
addition to nature,
the doctor said

Once upon a time I went
up yonder to Minnesota to find
the Connecticut warbler

(this may seem counter-intuitive
but it's where they go
so I did too)
I-35 in Duluth just peters out
deposits you on a tree-lined street
where the Superhighway ends

best to cross
the border on foot
now anyhow

The other end a different story:
snot-green milky substance
sloughing through a

colonia ("casas de cartón"),
a smell that'd "scare maggots off a gut-wagon"
proving people migrate to jobs

Ten minutes south of the river
you're on your own, no water
sewer no safety

Just north of the river, sun
burns gringos in the parking lot
waiting to take schooldesks across

I went another time as "avitourist"
Chihuahuan raven on the dump,
flotillas of screaming green parakeets

Nuestro national pájaro eats carrion
You get to define the "we"—
your privilege

bottled up
generic interlopers
additions to

headwinds   guns
a trickle of
declining

numbers
the super
road
kill

Incident at Cornfields
Gus Palmer

He caught the conch shell
blazing in the sun and with
his two-yearoold daughter he
gathered about the whitetail
deer and carried it streaming
from his shoulders and boned
through the brush. He dreamed
of peyote, not knowing which way
the putrid stone would throw him
in his gut. About him lay dry
sticks. He suspected where shells
came from and the oval-shaped beads.
They were not all stolen from the
place he thought. Rather, he caught
one of them cantering by the sea just
like the white-tail deer. He stretched
its blood over the stone to drape its
wound facedown in the sun, but the rain
fell and drained its image. He touched
the volcanic stone at the entrance of
his house but that too fell into a million
images. He dreamed of a fox in winter
blue when it issues from the rock each
black down of it. At noon, with its string of
coral beads it pads about his neck.
It breathes heavily of the air.
People look each day for its head to
become a watermelon they can
eat but he has them fooled as yet.
The corn separates itself into heads
when the white blossoms call
forth to the north god.

Indian Doctor
Gus Palmer

e̲:gàu dauia̲umà:dàu è dau:	This is a doctoring feather.
hàu: auhyàungàu è dau:	That's what it is.
e̲:dè dauia̲umxo: ø dau:?	This is a doctoring rock.
ha̲unê, haun dauia̲umxo: ø da̲u:mâu	No, it is not doctoring rock.
bo̲ibahetca gà dau:	It is lightning.
xo:jò èm dauia̲umgù:jàu	With medicine rocks I'll strike you.
a: xo:òbà gà dau:dètjò èm gu:jau	With feathers that are strong rocks I'll hit you.
bàt gu:jèjàu yan dauia̲u:màu	Take care. I'm making strong medcine for you.
kopqi ga kuljàu	I'll extract sick man out of you.
kopqi gà zànêhòljàu	I'll beat the hell out of sick man.
èm feaula̲:yîthàu	Your head will roll in pain.
bà feàula̲:yì:thàu	Both our heads will roll in pain.
e̲hàudèkì: ci:gòphe̲: gà dau:	This is our fearless day.

Indian Doctor 2
Gus Palmer

ja:dè en thàu:satca	His eyes shattered to pieces
gàu dè̲:he̲: ø au:a̲:gà qoptài	because he sits sleeplessly on a mountaintop.
Setqì	Bear Man.
auhyàudè ø dau:, èm jo̲:gà	That's him, you say.
ai:se̲ càu:gàu gà jau: haunde	He does it with ashes.
haunde ø zelbe dau:	He's outstanding.
bôt ha̲u:qàqì: dau:	After all he's an off-tribe.
ha̲u:òbà ø dau:	Ironlike.
auhyaudè ø dau:, èm jo̲:gà	Say that's who he is.
ø o̲:gàu	Such a fool!
am gà yauljàudè	One that acts coyote-like.
yaulàumqàjàiqì	Coyote Chief.
ba kòhài:bo̲:	Everybody, keep close eyes on him.
nàu haun bau thau:yauthàu	If you don't comply,
bau joljàu haya	I will banish you all.
bôt gà daui:zelbeil:dau:	Because it's dangerous medicine.

231

Augau Sep Gà Âigù (There Goes the Rain)
Gus Palmer

augau sep gà âigù	There goes the rain.
augau sep gà âigù	There goes the rain.
boibahepcacàu:gàu	Going along with lightning.
boibahepca càu:gàu	Going along with lightning.
pan ø aui:kòtjèà:	Sky comes a-whirling.
pan ø aui:kòtjèà:	Sky comes a-whirling.
jàujaui yá changacàu:màu	Father insists that I go.
yal ci:gòphe a ba:thàu	May I go fearlessly.
yal ci:gòphe a ba:thàu	May I go fearlessly.
jàujaui yá changacàu:màu:	Father insists that I go.
augau sep gà âigù	There goes the rain.
augau sep gà âigù	There goes the rain.
boibahepcacàu:gàu	Going along with lightning.
boibahepcacàu:gàu	Going along with lightning.

Upper Mississippi

Sonata for Tornado in EF-5 (Major): May 22, 2011, 5:41-6:13 pm
David Clewell

The people of Joplin were going about their daily lives on a Sunday evening: cooking supper, watching TV, walking the dog. And then came the whirlwind, nearly a mile wide and six miles long.

—Missouri Governor Jay Nixon

It was more like walking through The Twilight Zone *than walking down Main Street.*

—resident Eddie Atwood, the day after

for the citizens of Joplin—the dead and the living—victims and survivors of the single deadliest U.S. tornado in 62 years of record-keeping history

i

There's no one anywhere in town who's worried about much of anything on a breezy Sunday afternoon like this: Little League baseball in the park or a high school graduation or firing up the barbeque under a sky that's seemed so unreasonably clear all day, and even a last-minute run to the Gas-N-Go for cigarettes, sunglasses, one more cold six-pack just in case is truly no problem at all, even though the guy behind the counter won't stop talking about his to-die-for Saturday night, even now as he's getting louder, raising his voice so he can be heard over the rising noise of sirens going off as so often they do out of nowhere, here on the eastern edge of Tornado Alley, so yes, he hears them but no, not really, because the truth is: tornadoes have touched down hard only twice in the last forty years of sirens just like these. But this particular day's about to turn on everyone unthinkably fast, although they can't quite see it that way yet.

If a *watch* means conditions that could easily lend themselves to genuine, impending trouble, then most of us have carried on— weather and geography aside—under one kind of watch or another in effect for our whole lives. When that turns into an audible *warning* about whatever could be headed our way, in theory there should beat least a little time to prepare for the worst. But the fact is it's never sufficient. With hurricanes, there might be entire days to know each one by name, and still too many people remain unmoved. They end up stuck in the eye of the storm. With tornadoes? At best, twenty minutes—and that's with radar and subsequent sirens.

This is where folks are right now, I'm afraid—the headlong rush to hunker down, the trying to lie low. And blankets and pillows too, if they're handy. Forget about those solitary nights they didn't do nearly enough good. This time it's not about looking for comfort, but instead—in all likelihood—unmetaphorical, tangible flying debris.

ii.

They're standing five-deep in the dark of the Gas-N-Go's walk-in cooler, and what happens next is anyone's guess in a world this awfully small, reduced to nothing but soundtrack—a continuous deep rumbling, locomotive or jet engine or thundering waterfall, depending on who's trying to put such a primal sound into words—a crazy-strong 200-mile-an-hour wind that's barely an outside-world away. Not to mention the excruciating pressure.

It's best they can't see what's exploding off the shelves on the other side of the cooler door straining its hinges but hanging on, this near to bursting wide open: breath mints, magazines, candy bars, a flying wedge of Little Debbie no-expiration snack cakes. They can't see the façade of the Gas-N-Go breaking completely apart, going and suddenly gone. Can't see the power lines down, twitching out sparks that will light up the gas spewing from broken mains, homes and buildings on fire for miles. And they can't see how much of this city is currently up in the air: street signs, trash cans, windowpanes. WELCOME mats and floorboards. Whole families unceremoniously blown out of their living rooms.

In the cooler they're actually sweating it out, praying and crying and holding one another, wondering why these few minutes seem more than even an overblown lifetime. Someone's humming *Nearer, My God, to Thee*. Someone's singing *Over the Rainbow*. And

that radio preacher who'd wrongly predicted the end of the world
for last night—what if he'd somehow come closer than anyone
thought just this morning? A guy with no time for the Rapture
swears to hell with Harold Camping,

what matters is right here and now—a second disconcerting
round of hail. The ten-year-old kid, who's already had quite a day
at shortstop, who's also unabashedly something of a fifth-grade
weather geek, says hail forms at a tornado's leading edge, then
once more in its wake. They can't be sure he really knows what he
knows, but they have seen this kid's arm from deep in the hole, his
unerring long throw to first. They're afraid to say a word. They're
holding what's left of their breath in the dark and, with luck, in the
ever-widening, elemental quiet.

iii.

It's surely nothing less than a flat-out, windblown wonder that
anyone's left standing after the furious spinning winds down, after
the attendant howling mostly has subsided. And yet here they
come, those people stunned but slowly emerging from coolers,
from low-lying ditches, from the legendary southwest corner of
basements—some still dragging behind them the last-minute blan-
kets they found extra refuge in. Now it's these tentative baby steps,
as if for once, knee-deep in their lives, they truly have to start over,
making their separate ways back into a clearly more harrowing
world.

They knew the drill, and they know this aftermath-part-of-it too:
the deep breathing in, then the gradual exhalation. Soon they'll
be giving themselves the once-over, searching for cuts and abra-
sions. The bruises won't show up until later. There will be some
who would rather not look at the devastation behind them—in any
direction they're headed, not even a hundred yards from the end
of someone else's world—but they'll find themselves staring all the
same. In debris nearly three feet deep: torn-open animals minus
their stuffing, a Darth Vader Halloween mask, a birdcage, snap-
shots of birthdays and weddings, *Let It Bleed* and *Let It Be*
CDs, statues of St. Christopher in a jumble of steering wheels, a
crucifix driven into the trunk of the only tree holding its ground,

and a smaller unlikely miracle—a perfectly untangled Slinky coiled
tight at the top of a flight of stairs heading nowhere.

And as for the citizens alive
tonight in a city they can scarcely identify: everyone's a stroke-of-
luck survivor on the move, however slow their progress, looking
out for the others.

iv.

This is about the need to make sense
of what never will make sense, but still:
this is about the trying. This is not
about a return to normal. Although
the pressure has fallen to its more
natural level, there is always pressure.
In that way it's a lot like gravity.

This is by no means a metaphor—
not after 161 dead. The wind
has only died *down*. Not *out*.
There will always be wind. This is not
some allegorical *picking up the pieces*.
This means to gather what's hopelessly
broken on the ground—detritus
to sigh over, maybe, when salvage isn't
possible. This means getting on with it
as more than a figure of speech,
proceeding one arduous step at a time,
making discernible strides.

You can see
it's not exactly easy to negotiate
a realm this insistently literal.
But it's time to make something new
out of all this water and mud and
wind-swept straw, something notably
solid—not *like* a brick, but the brick
itself. Then another on top of that one,
the way the ancients built dwellings
and temples and tombs. We know this

because these things now and then
weathered the stormy forces of history—
so much of that broken beauty still
surviving, still undeniably here
in this world without end yet. Amen.

Still Life
Jeff Martin

The downpour came
Forcing worms from the ground
On a summer day

The rain stopped
The heat returned

Too quickly for the worms

There they are
Petrified
On sidewalks and driveways

Mid-motion
Half-curled

Like some miniature Pompeii.

What Claude Knew
Walter Bargen

Congested water lilies in the cultivated ponds
of gardens, under foot bridges that lead off
through trimmed trees and hedges to herbariums,

and down to canals lined with flared, wind-spangled
poplars: but always a broad flat leaf or two will
balance on stems high above the water, as if remembering

an earlier rising, but just now the pond looks like a madly
set table, a feast of rotting greens and yellows. Far from
such civilized gestures lilies hover on northern

lakes, and here the calm face of water is nudged
by pike and walleye, dimpled by sorties of dragonflies,
by a twisting nymph and circling beetle,

and the metamorphosis of clouds suspended
in the capillary tension as they slowly rear into
cumulus. Along the jagged shoreline spruce bristle in

their leaning reflections. In late light, half-submerged
boulders, ringed by bands of dried yellow pollen,
detail spring's fall. From behind the verdant

fragrance, a thrush sings clear as water that fills the lake
a second, a third time. Reaching over the canoe's
gunnel, an arm's shadow turns soggy. Fingers

stretch to grasp an amber resonance, as if reaching
through a museum window closed for years. The hand
doesn't come back but drifts off as the lake slips past.

Distant lily pads are the upturned palms of the others
who grabbed and held a lake's reflections, the wrinkled
stalks of their arms holding up an unexpected season.

Chain of Being
Walter Bargen

In this country men stop their trucks in the middle
of back roads and lean out of rusty, dented cabs,

sleeves rolled up to their elbows and propped on
rolled-down door windows as if to catch their heads

as they fall into long slow expressions of work, sadness,
and another beer. The beaks of their hats hold back

their eyes, as if there's a chance they might see too
far down the road where dust curls and crawls

behind a car turning in some other direction.
Their hats declare commerce and allegiance,

and today they talk used cars and the high price
for something worn out, rebuilt engines and guarantees

that are too short, transmissions and rear axles
grinding down, simple houses that take up a life's

time and more, the world bought and sold,
and so little between.

House of Turtle
Walter Bargen

I can't tell you where to start, maybe I don't know,
or maybe I'm simply not ready for the responsibility,
though it has nothing to do with not wanting to help,
nothing to do with all the possible guilts that sweep

over us for not having loved enough, or been present
enough, or even not having stopped the car and moved
the turtle off the road, and finding the flattened mess
when we returned, having watched in the rear-view

mirror another driver intentionally swerve. We must
take into account another time it was hopeless,
or just pointless, when we had not yet surrendered
hope, when the pond by the highway was drained

for a new apartment complex, the backhoe with its
claw sunk for the night into the breached embankment,
waiting for morning to again swallow another mouthful
of earth and spit it out. What more could be done,

the quitting-time traffic no longer able to dodge
those orphaned by the air, who crawled for other waters,
and over the asphalt the hundred or so moss-backed
shells were cracked and savaged flat by careless speed.

Perhaps this is just a warning, like the children standing
in a down pour shouting over whether running or walking
through the rain will leave them drier, even as the rain
falls harder, drenching their most refined arguments.

Good Place to Begin
Walter Bargen

The rain is always a good place to begin.
> After a summer's flooding, there are arguments
> and a sudden love for the desert light. But isn't
that the way it always is, if my house wasn't

floating furniture between rooms, comforting
> the murky water, and I wasn't the one counting
> the horizontal calendar of dried stains across
walls and windows, anticipating the rise and fall

of records and despair, and I wasn't listening
> to the reports of snakes hanging from kitchen
> ceilings and hogs crowded onto roofs waiting
for a second coming of the brown god perched

in the crowns of maples and the rescue boat cutting
> a wake through the trees, then I could open
> a palm calmly to the rain. But this unwanted
water is transcending everywhere, crossing bridges

and racing over roads, wearing down corn and soy-
> beans to their roots, and then, as if believing
> its own rapture, and after settling back into its old
ways, it leaves caskets blocking highways,

as if a fleet of fishing boats leaned on square
> keels, waiting for gentle tides of rain
> > to launch them and be swept away.

A Reappearance
Ted Kooser

Settled in nettles and brush by an old barn
near Nevada, Iowa, parked at a tilt
where the rusty wheel rims on the barn side
sunk into sod made spongy by sixty years
of rain and snowmelt, sits a semitrailer
holding up fourteen letters fading from red,
(Medium Red, Glidden's Bulletin Colors)
painted sans serif and canted to the right
to suggest speed, nearly all of the strokes
showing through from behind, some smooth
and skillful as if made with a light flourish,
lettered by J. Laverne Mullica, the others
more jerky and hesitant by apprentice
Ted Kooser, Jr., sixteen or seventeen then,
learning a skill from a master. Verne dead
more than forty years, the lofty shop
next to his house now someone's garage,
the cigarette smoke, paint fumes and thinner
wafted away, the portable Crosley with news
of the 'fifties shut off. Somewhere in there
he and I, side by side with quill brushes
and mahl sticks, shaping the letters, his wife,
Jane, calling us in for an afternoon break,
cigarettes burning away on our paint lids
behind us, red letters now washy and thin
on the trailer's side facing the highway,
NEVADA TRANSFER, and on the back side
shaded by the barn, the word nobody sees
as they hurry past, four letters: GONE.

Drops in the Funnel
Randy Brown

In the Fun Zone, west of the sheep barn,
the zip-line carnies eject by ones and twos
those fair-goers young/crazy/bored enough to pay $10 a head
just to slide down 130 feet of rope, from tower to ground.

Meanwhile, across the street, recruiters target able-bodied passersby
for push-up fun and prizes, handing out water bottles and bumper stickers,
barking that Uncle Sam will toss you out of a perfectly good aircraft
absolutely free-of-charge, if you'll just step right up and raise your hand.

No felonies, please.
No neck tattoos.
No drug users.
No drop-outs.

Say it takes 100 names and numbers for 10 good leads:
Work those 10 hard, and you might get one enlistment—
one that might still require a couple of waivers to boot.
Just hope they don't have asthma, or psych out at Basic.

Our tan trucks and tents are caked with dust,
and the wet State Fair heat feels worse than Iraq and the 'Stan
        rolled together.
Still, there are kids lining up to play in the turrets of our Humvees,
and put their butts in the gunner's sling, like we once did.

So God bless Midway America, its fried cheese and funnel cakes,
and every sweaty, dough-faced dreamer in blue jeans
who thinks that parachutist's wings and a uniform
might just be a ticket out of fly-over country.

Stand up, hook them up, and shuffle them toward the door.

Fighting Seasons
Randy Brown

Even a city boy from Eastern Iowa
follows the markets, like sports, on the A.M. radio
and has a vague sense of the harvests to come.

Feeder calves and pork-belly futures, forecasts for soybeans and corn
fill our diner conversations and our mouths
like bushel-bags of baseball stats, ideals and speculations.

The Cubs might finally do it this fall. And El Niño could make a comeback.
Into this familiar world, armed with coffee and pie,
a waitress gently probes toward our war: *Heard anything from your sons?*

Floods and droughts, blizzards and winds
are no strangers to the plains. We work the land,
the land works us. We do our jobs. Good weather either happens,
       or it doesn't.

It is winter in Eastern Afghanistan, but spring is coming.
There are no crops of poppies there—that's down south.
News is, the fighting will soon resume. At least, that's what the
       papers say.

Maybe this year will finally be our year.

Interstate
William Trowbridge

(I35 North, Iowa)

The last thing you remember seeing: that billboard
advertising advertising on a rise just past
the Swaledale turnoff; now it's MASON CITY
NEXT 2 EXITS, patches of old snow melting
on the shoulders, a Perkins, a Wendy's.
How long have you been missing? Ten Miles?
Twenty? And how'd you do it, with your family
right there thinking something more than protoplasm
steered them around the curves and slowpokes?
Are they so accustomed to your lack by now
that you can disappear unnoticed—no wires,
mirrors—before their very eyes? Or did they, too,
drift beyond the car, afterwards solely occupied
by soulless ones or ones with souls suspended
or displaced by, who knows, some ectoplasmic
hitchhikers hopping easy as you please from car
to car on their way to this year's International
Convention of the Dead in Winnipeg? And when
your ghost slipped out of Iowa, what was your state?
Weltschmerz? Ennui? or simply southern Minnesota,
your haste to reach the Clinic whisking you ahead
to Rochester? Maybe you died and went to heaven,
only to be dropped back here, on cruise control,
hoping the doctors can scope out just what makes
you worry so, when everybody's passing through
those walls to someplace else, turning Jacob Marley
or Ulalume and back twenty, fifty times a week,
a day. Who's got time to count? Besides, here's
the Northwood turnoff, 20 miles past Mason City.

The Road
William Trowbridge

As kids, we watched it
   out the windshield
      of the family sedan,

spooling at us
   from the flat horizon,
      expanding from that

vanishing point
   we learned about
      in art class—magnetic,

rushing past,
   pulling us toward
      its peephole tease.

Behind the wheel
   at last, we sipped
      its danger, fed

on it clues
   never outgrew
      its leitmotif.

When we pack up,
   the tires still sing
      Gone. Over and out

as we drive off, suckers
   for the high roll
      of center line and landscape,

shedding cares,
   shedding cells,
      half-hypnotized

by expectation's
   slippery caress,
      half-awake

to the chance of
   ditch or power pole,
      of kingdom come.

Lost on Maps
Tony Spicer

After Neruda's "Ode to a Violin in California"

I am a red man's hungry violin
imperfectly made, eyes ragged, scraping
dead grass or rabbit dung from
aluminum cans along roadsides.
O long years wanting my teachers again
among prairie fires or deltas as far away
from me now as pale continents or Mars.
Will I ever see them again, their cotton fog
lowlands at dawn? Hear glowing, high-strung
whippoorwill notes? We may long for what we've
never seen, but cry out meteoric strains
for what's lost. While we sleep or gather
clothing to launder--the two feel
mostly the same--rivers we renamed
for love or mothers run down our necks
so slightly off key they wash sand
from the bars and flood beyond the Glaize's banks
while fretless mountains cough their ancient songs.

Indelible Ink
Tony Spicer

But it's history, you see. Not the usual complaints.
I own no gold. Never gold. Bathed in blood,
invasive hands dig soil from my heart, then eat both.
Mountainside and valley, mutilated timbers crush
smoldering cabins while my grandfathers,
grandmothers, tall ghosts, stomp and sing
without joy. And their grandmothers walk on,
or remain and chew off their own tongues, resigned
to visions, to secret, living feathers
 in a red cedar box wrapped in a blanket.

And it's ever-present, you see. I do not need it to remember,
but wear a black star scraped into my arm. Prime real
estate, the artist said. Blood and ink under his gun.
He started quickly, just another "nautical," then
sighed, "oh, man," when I told him why, and found
his steadied, more attentive strokes for my fire, lightening,
for the single feather's weight on my shoulder.

Legend
Gregory Stapp

These lines are freeways,
highways, interstates, paths,
dotted lengths, longitudinal lines
like 35°15′, prime meridian,
Tropic of Cancer, black spots,
towns, stars—cities in symbolic shapes.
Along Route 66, in Carthage perhaps,
a crumb of dirt constitutes a city,
period, mole, granule,
grain of sand in your palm among a million—
I'm 1/80,000th of that speck. 0.0000125x.

These lines drive a freeway,
become a wide river: Zambezi,
South Platte, flood gates, borderline,
division of state, or state of mind. The Ob,
azure ribbon, draws a river, a string, untied
strand between knotted state lines,
a bookmark in nation story—
I'm 1/16th of an inch of that line. 0.0625x.

These lines span the flooding river.
These lines are a notion: political moods,
where hammers swing, graveyards,
names of places renamed, a crossing,
bridge, vista, point of view, projections—
the splitting of a sphere into an orange peel,
a world flattened on the wall. Key:

your thumb-length equals 2000 miles,
fingerprints rise 8500 feet above sea level,
your foot spans the eastern hemisphere.
You could destroy your enemies
with a match, erase lines to change
borders, or make oceans mountains.

These lines form a notion.
These lines cancel the world

onto paper, from a mass of stone,
water and gas to color-coordinated countries,
solid line abstractions, daylight at all times,
cloudless, weatherless, and without current.
Scale: 1:33,000,000. I lie flat, arms spread
like a man-made canal, world-sized.

What We Did Instead
Jennifer Boyden

One personal reproductive theory
is that
      if my husband and I had installed a device
under our bed, programmed so a thrust-
activated movement sensor
would trigger a voice
that would cry out "war, war, war"—if we'd done
that—we wouldn't have
our daughter now.

My husband, who has one heart that shines
on the table of all possible hearts,
would have had to fold up his penis
and put it away until the sensor broke
or we forced ourselves to pretend
that the word *war* was just another word
for *shake your ass,* or *hold it there,* or *next time
let's eat chicken while we do this.*

I noticed in the paper
how the runway models were thin again
and black-eyed
      in clothing so thin it wouldn't get stolen
in a refugee camp. I think it means something

that lately when I put on my shoes
I think: Do these work
for fleeing a homeland? Are they too easy
to steal from my exhausted feet?
Lately, my boots lace to the knees.

Airplanes were exploding our towers
so we could get on with war.
We hadn't installed a sensor machine,
but we heard war in every door opening, every bit
into fruit. We were slick with it.

We did not install
the machine. What we did instead
was go to Minnesota in the middle of winter
where it was so cold
the fish we pulled up through the ice holes
were green logs with eyes.

We cut them open
and threw their guts at winter
where the birds ate them. We were there
to visit my family, all just in from the frozen lake
of the blue-green fish,
and I was a few beers down with an egg
on its way
and for a moment as I stood with my husband
among my people
who were breading the fish
and humming and slapping their thighs
by the fire, there was no war anywhere.
I mean this is what we had
at that moment:

food, fire, a game
on the wood table where people pressed
buzzers and flipped the timer, laughing. We turned away

to head upstairs to the room we shared.
We closed the door. We laid down
where no one had thought to install a machine,
and we made one child and had to watch
her open as the world entered bit by bit,
and the world was sharp where she was best.

The retail index reveals there is something sexy
about how the models are nearly dead with hunger.

In our bed, we now read books and hear
a voice that, if we turn our heads properly,
sounds like it's calling us off to sleep.

I Try to Cancel My Credit Card
Matt Guenette

I try to cancel my credit card.

While I wait, I imagine, in every megachurch along I-35, from
Duluth to Laredo, my Social Security number broadcast on the
large technological displays as part of some watered down liturgy
on psychology, patriotism, and, most importantly fundraising.

I've been told Jesus, who never got married or held
a steady job or permanent address, wants me to carry on
in his image: classical, cool, miraculous, even sensual.

I've been told Jesus, who was sure his mother was a virgin
and who never had to empty a trash-can or mow the lawn, means
to point me in the direction of the lowest, most competitive rates.

What could be more biblical than, say, a debt, which is nothing
more than a choice, and a predicament, symptomatic of some
other issue that presumes upon the future like a boss that thinks
he knows everything?

What could be more biblical than, say, a donation charged to my
card, without my consent, that takes 33 years
and thousands to pay off?

If it could, my credit score would ding so loud
they would name a five-alarm chili after me in Oklahoma City, a
place where the cost of living is low, and gas
is cheap, and where, once, I felt like a pebble
dropped into a lake, when, in a bar surrounded by cowboys, and
sun-burnt suburbs and fields, I
lost my wallet.

Electric Snakes

Adrian Louis

1. Shame & tragedy have entered my shabby life. Today I saw another retired professor at the day-old bread store.

2. Fuck these little Minnesota rabbits in my yard. I bought the little shits a bag of baby carrots that they chose to spurn. I want the jackrabbits of my youth. Jackrabbits seem only to live west of the Missouri River. Jackrabbits are not rabbits. They are hares. Folks, they come by their name because their huge ears resemble jackass (donkey) ears. So, fuck these Minnesota rabbits. Class dismissed.

3. Here's a headline I yearn to see: "Kanye Caught Cornholing Caitlyn."

4. 75280ZDWIRENONV82. I was the small circle imprisoned inside the steel square. Far away now, thank God, but then, that sultry autumn night on the far cusp of youth with not a single gray hair, yours truly screwed the pooch.

5. Last year there were seven thousand wild Indians or more camped out on the Standing Rock Reservation & I thought of Trump's blonde hair & I felt the dark wind blowing in from the Little Big Horn. Winter, bleak & endless winter is in the air.

Skinology
Adrian Louis

Yellow roses, wild roses,
their decades of growth,
a fierce fence between
the drunkenness
of my neighbors
& me.

φφφ
I have known
some badass Skins.
Clichéd bad-to-the-bone
Indians who were maybe
not bad but just broke,
& broken for sure.

φφφ
Late winter, late night,
a gentle rapping, a tapping
on my chamber door...
some guy selling a block
of commodity cheese
for five bucks.

φφφ
You climbed a tree,
sat there for hours
until some kind voice
called you back home.
You unfolded your wings,
took to the air & smashed
into earth. They hauled
you to ER, then Detox
where they laughed
at your broken wings.

φφφ
Once, I thought
I saw eagles soar,

loop & do the crow hop
in the blue air while
the sun beat the earth
like a drum, but I was
disheveled & drinking
those years.

φφφ
Indians & the internet.
Somewhere, sometime.
Whenever a Messiah
Chief is born, jealous
relatives will drag him
down like the old days
only instantly now.

φφφ
In a brutal land
within a brutal land
with corrupt leaders
& children killing themselves
we know who is to blame.
But, we are on a train,
a runaway train & we
don't know what to do.

φφφ
The good earth,
the sun blazing down,
us in our chones, butts
stuck in inner tubes,
floating down a mossy
green river, speechless,
stunned silent with joy
& sobriety & youth,
oh youth.

φφφ
She smiled at me
& got off her horse.
She smelled of leather
& sweat & her kiss has
lasted me fifty years.

φφφ
Bad Indians do
not go to hell.
They are marched
to the molten core
of the sun & then
beamed back to
their families,
purified, whole
& Holy as hell.

The Motherland
Adrian Louis

Election Night, 2016

Pallid folks, both guided
& misguided, bump uglies
& exchange vows against
a backdrop of dirges sung
by millions of dark men
seething behind steel bars.
Pallid folks are bored with
the old songs of pain & are
thankful that the cold heart
of democracy, sliced thinly,
has fed them for centuries.
Sieg Heil, Mama-jammers.
Sieg Heil, Flim-flammers.

The Necessity of Empty Places
Taylor Brorby

For Carolyn Raffensperger

As we drive south from Minneapolis towards Ames,
Renee reminds me *that there's nothing here,*
nothing along the soft folds of earth, neatly packed
rows of high—green & low—green—corn & soybeans—
nothing but acres of farmland, blue dome of sky.
But I remind her that not so long ago an ocean of grass
roiled here—big bluestem, Canada wild rye, whose
caterpillar body lolled back & forth in the breeze.
We are in the land of grasses.

There's a story, I say, as she puffs balls of smoke
out of the car. Her purple hair thrashes in the wind.
*A story that Melville was intimidated by the tallgrass
prairie when it whipped in the afternoon breeze—
prairie, more threatening than his mighty Atlantic.*

She exhales & adjusts her sunglasses.
But there's nothing here but pigs & the smell of shit.
Forbs & soil, I tell her, soil the color of Dutch cocoa,
soil secured by a wash of grass, until we arrived
with plows—metal that cut & scraped, turned
& divided Iowa into an ocean of profit.
We thought we had to feed the world, I say,
when we really meant to feed our pocketbooks.

on leavings
JL Jacobs

For Thomas A. Jones (1953-2017)

How do you / eat a dead man's / last fish
Walleye / carried back from Canada / we fried last / our beloved
country doctor's fillets. / Penultimate bite / he left me a bone
for my keening.

****

on creek bottoms

blue / moon time
thunder rumbles distantly
the tides call
all
to their knees
all might
gone
all weapons
aside...
all feeble
and tremble
inside
your call
your attentive
love-ing
make all seem
a bedrock
I answered
with quartz
and more bedded rock—
Apache tears
& crazy lace
and prayed
that the seeming/seaming
might "be".

A Concrete Ribbon
Marcie Rendon

A concrete ribbon leaving Gitchigami
Hangs down the middle of Aki

Driving south through Minnesota soy and corn fields
Ancient spirits, sitting in the backseat,
long to travel Mississippi flood waters.
They whisper stories in my ear of a
Living waterway slightly to the east,
Raging waters, carrying mud
And giant catfish South.

But I stay the course
Concrete roadway, immobile, steady
Even through Tornado Alley.

Round about Osage country
Ancient riders in the back tell me they are carsick,
They say the spirits who travel with them
(I wonder how they all crowded into my backseat and do they have
        their seat belts on?)
Are complaining.
They say Sorrow has pulled them from the car windows
and they have become tumbleweeds
rolling in the ditches where vortex winds are
Littered with the words and sounds
Of trafficked women and children.
They beg me to pull over at the nearest truck stop,
Tell me to open all the car doors
Release the sorrow and let the others roll back in.
I needed gas anyways.

Later, south of Oklahoma City
The stainless steel rest stop water fountain
Squirts a two-foot high stream of water.
Shaking water from hair and t-shirt
I hear the gulps of parched throats and
Murmurs of Miigwetch, Miigwetch.
Moccasin-ed feet, that only I can see
Leave damp, subtle tracks on concrete sidewalk,

Lead me back to rental that will take us farther south.
I wipe the sweat from my brow, shift the car into drive,
As I wonder why they ride with me
When with a twist of air They could reach Laredo
Faster than a thought.

I forget they can hear unspoken words.
The Oldest of the Oldest, comfortably wrapped in a Pendleton coat, says
"This journey from Gitchigami to the Red, sister of the
Northern Red, is a long and ancient journey. A trip like this re-
quires
Some to guide,
some to remember and remind,
some to protect, and
(pointing lips at Ancient One carefully applying red lipstick,
        wrinkled eyes squinting into pocket
mirror pulled from leather purse on lap)
some along just for the ride."

I continue south. Nothing solid. Nothing immobile.

Sawhorse
Eric Chandler

I almost killed Phil more than once.
I backed out of my driveway and braked for the
Green Bay Packers jacket and white cane
taking Tuffy the West Highland terrier for a walk
in the dark during a snowstorm.
It was all the same to blind Phil.
He messed around across the alley
in his garage with his power tools
while his wife Marty tended the flower gardens and
the giant rhubarb plant.
He made me a pair of sawhorses.
Two-by-fours with remnants of red and green paint
held together with long deck screws.
Still amazed he didn't cut off
one of his fingers in the
permanent dark.

Not sure what to do with them,
I took them to the cabin.
They ended up holding the boatlift
above the frozen water.
Eight legs immobilized in the white
with their heavy load.
In the same spot when the spring waves
lapped at the now-gray wood.
Sentinels in the ice,
year after year.
Indestructible.

I visited Phil when his insides failed.
I saw him hold his hand in the air.
Kind of waving it, never able to see me,
—not before, not now—
from that bed in hospice.
Marty, said, "He wants to hold your hand."
I should've known something was up when, earlier,
he gave my kids all his fishing poles
and me all his bottles of brandy.

I see Marty walk with Tuffy every day.
Badasses out in all the snow and ice
that Duluth delivers,
just like Phil.

Last year, one of the sawhorses was swept away.
Just disappeared.
What good is one sawhorse?
I went to the cabin with two new plastic ones.
They joined the boatlift team with the sole survivor.
I stomped through the knee-deep snow this winter to check on things.
The plastic swaybacked under the load while
Phil's sawhorse stood stoic surveying the snow.
Bearing the weight like Atlas.

Slippage
Kimberly Blaeser

How many times lost
in the apparitions
of white dragon breath,
moon slipping in and out
behind the dancing fringe of fog?
Somewhere on the water's edge
trapped in the thin, horizon line
between dark-sky Thunderbirds
and legendary spiked sea serpents,
lonely souls yearn or keen
on too solid ground.
Finding the vaporous shore
where every solid thing
becomes unseen,
where water fills air,
and the great panther still roars
against the rocks.
Mishibijiw
summoner of the storms,
your tail a vision like copper,
riding the seiche and surge
sinking us, jagged and heavy as rock,
in the uncanny call of night.
Three quadrillion gallons of water—
never enough for escape.
Your lair deep, deeper...
1,333 icy deepest feet down,
past lost schooners, sunken freighters,
in the miasma of myth
where the Emperor and the Edmund Fitzgerald
now waltz together sweetly
in currents of *Gichigami*.
Each lost legend summoned
swallowed like the Nelson.
Somewhere submerged, ship wheels still
then turn, the memory of squalls
bring splash and hiss echoing to shore
to wash the feet of wayfarers.

Who knows the lull and longing?
This ancient scented language
is sand, shells, and spray,
the call of sea gulls and mystery,
is underwater monsters, craggy cliffs,
and, yes, our many drowned kingdoms.

The Way We Love Something Small
Kimberly Blaeser

Here delicate ink of mayflies
on the glazed gray pottery of lake.
There the dipping nib of the iris
graceful lilac curves at water's edge.

Now the lilac plunged into deep purple refraction;
elongated mayfly bodies splayed—
the stained glass window of their wings
flutters a transparency, repeats repeats repeats
across some glass surface of being.

How our eyes count infinity—
how exquisitely it eludes.

The Ritual of Wishing Hands
Kimberly Blaeser

1945 and you stand ship side
a man's body all angles and anger—
myth poking out at your hip,
at the jut of the shoulder.
Yes. A photo. Inherited bones.
How they meander the map of our body,
each dark flap of hair a flag of defiance—
scribbling over the legend, the key.

Each year we drive between water and city
gichigami a harbor—like the memory of you,
like stories carved deeper with each telling—
roads rutted with history of our ancestors:
those who traveled through, those left behind.
Hands up for wishes—we've lifted them
years on end like Atlas on the western edge.
But here Gaia in our northern corridor
spills different stories: *anima mundi.*
Soul hold, again and again hold
child's hands in this dark Duluth tunnel.

In the long stretches between daylight
sometimes the shadows crowd between us
dark and broken stories of urban *wiindigoo*;
sometimes we hold our breath too long
like believing and disbelieving is only a game.
In this strange ritual of wishing hands
we flatten fingers against the sky
travel this spine of asphalt—
this dream passage to almost there.

You carried shriveled oranges
in relocation's dark pockets,
carried bruise blue veins and knotted muscles
home to crowded reservation tables.
You spilled the blood coins at taverns
then determinedly unmapped the way
to renamed city waterfronts—
we followed your stories just the same.

Summers on I-35 I believe in a world of betweens:
I am a dock, a wharf, a quay—
a port suspended between shades of blue.
I am a birch, a pine, a notched spine—
leaf green and copper rooted between earth and sky.
Perhaps Black Elk's red roads and black converge here
where the tired back of Turtle's earth
and the immense sky world of Thunderbirds
meet in the everyday prayers of tiny hands
reaching up to the roof of speeding cars.

Contributor Notes

Sly Alley is a writer of poetry and short-fiction whose debut collection, *Strong Medicine*, won the 2017 Oklahoma Book Award for Poetry. He is currently writing his next poetry collection from a fortified shack in Tecumseh, Oklahoma.

Hala Alyan is a Palestinian American writer and clinical psychologist whose work has appeared in *The New York Times*, *Guernica* and elsewhere. Her poetry collections have won the Arab American Book Award and the Crab Orchard Series. Her debut novel, *Salt Houses*, was published by Houghton Mifflin Harcourt in 2017, and was the winner of the Arab American Book Award and the Dayton Literary Peace Prize. Her poetry collection, *The Twenty-Ninth Year*, was released by Houghton Mifflin Harcourt. Her latest novel, *The Arsonists' City*, was published by Mariner Books in 2021.

Andrea Alzati (México, 1989) studied Latin American Literature in Universidad Iberoamericana. Her poem "Anatomía del huevo" has been published in two anthologies in Mexico and Spain. She has published the poetry books *Animal Doméstico* (Juan Malasuerte Editores, México, 2017) and *Todos mis quchillos* (Komorebi Ediciones, Valdivia, 2019) and the mixed media book *Algo tan oscuro que no tiene nombre* (Dharma Books & Publishing, México, 2018). Some of her works can be seen in www.andreaalzati.com.

Consuelo Alzati was born in Mexico City in 1982. She obtained a BA in Contemplative Psychology from Naropa University, in Boulder, Colorado in the United States. She has dedicated most of her professional life to teaching English to Spanish speaking children. She also studied photography at the university, as well as in the Center of Photographic Arts Saul Serrano. Photography has been her preferred artistic expression for the last 20 years.

After forty-one years in public education in four states and one year as marketing director for a small hospital in southern Kansas, Doc Arnett retired and returned to northeast Kansas in 2020. He and Randa, his wife of thirty-plus years, share eight surviving children and thirty grandchildren. And two horses. A native of Kentucky, Doc worked in Kansas for nearly twenty years and has lived there for eleven years. A bi-vocational minister since 1975, he enjoys singing and playing guitar, remodeling, biking, mud runs, hiking, cabinet and furniture making, and writing. In the late 80's and early 90's, he co-published with William Jolliff, *The Rolling Coulter,* a journal of agrarian poetry.

Paul Austin's collection *Notes on Hard Times* was published by Village Books Press. His work has appeared in such publications as *This Land, Sugar Mule, Oklahoma Review, More Monologues by Men,* and *Newport Review.* His poems have also been included in *Speak Your Mind,* the 2019 anthology of *Woody Guthrie Poets, Bull Buffalo and Indian Paintbrush: the Poetry of Oklahoma, Behind the mask: Haiku in the Time of Covid-19,* and *Jerry Jazz Musician. Late Night Conspiracies,* a collection of his writings was performed with jazz ensemble at New York's Ensemble Studio Theatre. He has written for and about the theatre in essays, poetry and plays, including *Spontaneous Behavior, the Art of Character Acting.*

Walter Bargen has published 25 books of poetry. Recent books include: *My Other Mother's Red Mercedes* (Lamar University Press, 2018), *Until Next Time* (Singing Bone Press, 2019), *Pole Dancing in the Night Club of God* (Red Mountain Press, 2020), and *You Wounded Miracle,* (Liliom, 2021). He was appointed the first poet laureate of Missouri (2008-2009).

Jim Barnes was Oklahoma Poet Laureate for 2009 and 2010. He is the author of a dozen volumes of poetry, including *Visiting Picasso* (University of Illinois Press, 2007) and *Sundown Explains Nothing: New and Selected Poems* (Stephen F. Austin State University Press, 2019). His individual poems have appeared widely in national and international publications, including *The Nation, The American Scholar, Kenyon Review,* and *Poetry Wales.* His honors include a National Endowment for the Arts Fellowship, as well as residential fellowships from the Rockefeller Foundation (Bellagio, Italy), the Camargo Foundation (Cassis, France), the Villa Walberta (Feldafing, Germany), and the Fulbright Program (Lausanne, Switzerland). He is the translator of Dagmar Nick's *Summons and Sign and Numbered Days.*

Roy Beckemeyer has lived within the I-35 corridor for three-quarters of his life, first in San Antonio, Texas, later in Wichita, Kansas, his current home. He is a retired engineer and scientific journal editor.

Beckemeyer's latest poetry collection is *Mouth Brimming Over* (Blue Cedar Press, 2019). *Stage Whispers* (Meadowlark Books, 2018) won the 2019 Nelson Poetry Book Award. *Amanuensis Angel* (Spartan Press, 2018) comprised ekphrastic poems inspired by depictions of angels in works of modern art. *Music I Once Could Dance To* (Coal City Press, 2014) was a 2015 Kansas Notable Book.

Kimberly Blaeser, former Wisconsin Poet Laureate, is the author of five poetry collections including *Copper Yearning, Apprenticed to Justice,* and *Résister en dansant/Ikwe-niimi: Dancing Resistance.* An Anishinaabe activist and environmentalist from White Earth Reservation, Blaeser is a Professor of English and Indigenous studies at University of Wisconsin–Milwaukee, an MFA faculty member for the Institute of American Indian Arts in Santa Fe, and founding director of In-Na-Po—Indigenous Nations Poets.

Bruce Bond is the author of twenty-eight books including, most recently, *Plurality and the Poetics of Self* (Palgrave, 2019), *Words Written Against the Walls of the City* (LSU, 2019), *Scar* (Etruscan, 2020), *Behemoth* (New Criterion Prize, Criterion Books), *The Calling* (Parlor, 2021), and *Patmos* (Juniper Prize, UMass, 2021). Three books are forthcoming: *Liberation of Dissonance* (Nicholas Shaffner Award for Literature in Music, Schaffner Press, 2022), *Choreomania* (MadHat, 2022), and *Invention of the Wilderness* (LSU, 2022). His work has appeared in numerous journals and anthologies, including seven editions of *Best American Poetry*. Presently he is Regents Emeritus Professor of English at the University of North Texas.

Paul Bowers lives on a small farm in northwestern Oklahoma. He teaches writing and literature at Northern Oklahoma College in Enid, and is the author of a short story collection, *Like Men, Made Various,* and two poetry collections: *The Lone, Cautious, Animal Life,* and *Occasional Hymns*. His third poetry collection, *Ten Acres of the Universe,* will be released in 2022.

Jennifer Boyden is author of two books of poetry: *The Declarable Future* (Four Lakes Prize in Poetry) and *The Mouths of Grazing Things* (Brittingham Prize in Poetry), as well as the novel *The Chief of Rally Tree*. Growing up in Minnesota near I35 meant it was always making promises about *Somewhere Else*. Jennifer traveled its distances in cars made to fail. I35 taught her beauty of hospitality in an ice storm, how to save a deer after midnight, which neon lights correlate to a superior burger, and how a shovel, a map, and a bottle of water make us invincible. Though Jennifer now writes, teaches, and is a college counselor in the west, the landscapes of I35 continue to do their work wherever she goes.

Timothy Bradford is the author of the poetry collection *Nomads with Samsonite*, a Lecturer in the Expository Writing Program at the University of Oklahoma, a co-director of the Mark Allen Everett Poetry Series, and a volunteer with the Writers Guild at Joseph Harp Correctional Center in Lexington, Oklahoma, just twenty minutes east of I35.

Taylor Brorby is the author of *Crude: Poems, Coming Alive: Action and Civil Disobedience,* co-editor of *Fracture: Essays, Poems and Stories on Fracking in America.* His work has been supported by the MacDowell Colony, the National Book Critics Circle, and the Stone Barns Center for Food and Agriculture. He serves on the editorial boards of Hub City Press and Terrain.org, and is a contributing editor at *North American Review.* His memoir *Boys and Oil* is forthcoming from Liveright/W.W. Norton. Find him at taylor-brorby.com.

Nathan Brown is an author, singer-songwriter, and award-winning poet living in Wimberley, Texas. He served as Poet Laureate of Oklahoma in 2013/14. He's published over 20 books of poetry and memoir. His most recent collection of poems is *In the Days of Our Resilience,* the fourth in a series now known as the *Pandemic Poems Project,* that deals with the year of the pandemic. And his new travel memoir *Just Another Honeymoon in France: A Vagabond at Large,* is a wonderful romp through Paris and the Bordeaux region. An earlier book, *Two Tables Over,* won the Oklahoma Book Award.

Randy Brown embedded with his former Iowa Army National Guard unit as a civilian journalist in Afghanistan, May-June 2011. A 20-year veteran with one overseas deployment, he subsequently authored the 2015 poetry collection *Welcome to FOB Haiku: War Poems from Inside the Wire.* He also co-edited the 2019 anthology *Why We Write: Craft Essays on Writing War.* He is a three-time poetry finalist in the Col. Darron L. Wright Memorial Writing Awards at

Line of Advance, and the 2018 "Untold Stories" winner at *Flyway: Journal of Writing & Environment*. His poetry and non-fiction have appeared widely in print and on-line, including in Belt Publishing's 2019 anthology *Midwest Architecture Journeys*, *Midwestern Gothic, Backchannels*, and *So It Goes: The Literary Journal of the Kurt Vonnegut Museum and Library*. As "Charlie Sherpa," he blogs about modern war poetry at www.fobhaiku.com, and about military-themed writing at www.aimingcircle.org.

Marcello Hernandez Castillo's most recent book is *Children of the Land: a Memoir* (Harper Collins). He is also the author of the poetry collections *Cenzontle*, winner of the A. Poulin, Jr. prize (BOA editions) in 2018, and *Dulce*, winner of the Drinking Gourd Prize (Northwestern University Press). He lives in Northern California where he serves as visiting assistant professor at St. Mary's College and teaches for the Ashland University Low-Res MFA program.

R. T. Castleberry's work has appeared in *Roanoke Review, Santa Fe Literary Review, Comstock Review, Green Mountains Review, The Alembic, Silk Road,* and *Argestes*. It's been featured in the anthologies: *Travois: An Anthology of Texas Poetry, TimeSlice, The Weight of Addition, Anthem: A Tribute to Leonard Cohen* and Blue Milk's anthology, *Dawn*.

Marlys Cervantes is a writer of poetry, inspiration, and creative non-fiction, as well as a photographer of trees and an actor in community theater. Cervantes serves as the chair of the Humanities and Communication department at Cowley College in Arkansas City, Kansas, where she teaches literature and writing courses. She and her sweetheart Jose live in Ponca City, Oklahoma, where they cultivate plants and flowers to draw bees, birds, and butterflies to their backyard.

Eric Chandler is the author of *Kekekabic* (Finishing Line Press, 2022) and *Hugging This Rock: Poems of Earth & Sky, Love & War* (Middle West Press, 2017). His writing has appeared in *Northern Wilds, Grey Sparrow Journal, The Talking Stick, Flying Magazine, The Thunderbird Review, O-Dark-Thirty, Line of Advance, Consequence Magazine, The Deadly Writers Patrol, PANK,* and *Columbia Journal*. Chandler was nominated for a Pushcart Prize in 2014 for creative nonfiction. He's a three-time winner of the Col. Darron L. Wright Award for poetry. A retired US Air Force veteran of the active duty and the Minnesota Air National Guard, he flew 145 combat missions and over 3000 hours in the F-16. Eric is a husband and father who cross-country skis as fast as he can in Duluth, Minnesota.

David Clewell (1955-2020) is the author of ten collections of poems—most recently, *Almost Nothing To Be Scared Of* (University of Wisconsin Press, 2016)—and two book-length poems. His work has appeared regularly in a wide variety of national magazines and journals—including *Harper's, Poetry, The Georgia Review, Kenyon Review,* and *New Letters*—and is represented in more than fifty anthologies. Among his honors are several book awards: two Four Lakes Poetry Prizes (for *Taken Somehow by Surprise* and *Almost Nothing To Be Scared Of*), the Felix Pollak Poetry Prize (for *Now We're Getting Somewhere*), and a National Poetry Series selection (*Blessings in Disguise*). He served as Poet Laureate of Missouri from 2010-2012. Clewell has worked as a professional wrestler, circus laborer, and boardwalk weight-guesser. He currently labors as a professor of English and director of the creative writing program at Webster University in St. Louis. His collection of Charlie the Tuna iconography is currently the largest in private curatorship.

Laura Da' is a poet and teacher. A lifetime resident of the Pacific Northwest, Da' studied creative writing at the University of Washington and The Institute of American Indian Arts. Da' is Eastern Shawnee. She is the author of *Tributaries,* winner of the American Book Award, and I*nstruments of the True Measure,* winner of the Washington State Book Award. Da' lives near Renton with her husband and son.

Brian Daffron grew up in northeast Arkansas and moved to Oklahoma in 1998. His publications include *Indian Country Today, Native American Times, Oklahoma Gazette, OKC Business, Tribal College Journal,* and *American Indian Art.* Two of his essays appear in *When Dream Bear Sings: Native Literature of the Southern Plains* (2018) by University of Nebraska Press. He lives in Norman, Oklahoma, with his wife, Maya, and their four children: Chado, Kateri, Matthias, and Frankie.

A self-proclaimed desert rat, Chuck Etheridge was raised in El Paso, Texas. After a stint in the US Navy keeping the coast of Southern

California safe from the threat of enemy invasion, he attended the University of Texas at El Paso and Texas Christian University. In addition to his time in the service, he has worked as an actor, a convenience store clerk, a Rent-a-Poet, and a catalog copy writer before finding respectable employment as an English teacher, first at McMurry University and, later, at Texas A&M University-Corpus Christi. His poetry, fiction, and creative non-fiction have been published in a variety of reviews and anthologized in a number of books, and he has written two plays that have been produced. His first two novels, *Border Canto* and *The Desert After Rain,* were published by Fine Tooth Press. A motion picture based on his Border Canto Trilogy is in development. His comic novel *Chagford Revisited* was just published in the UK in 2021 and is available in the States on Amazon.

Charles Evans is a poet, artist and social services worker in Minneapolis. He can be found at www.charlesdevans.com.

Todd Fuller is co-editor of *Level Land* and serves as curator of the Western History Collections at the University of Oklahoma. He is the author of *60 Feet Six Inches and Other Distances from Home: the (Baseball) Life of Mose YellowHorse* (Holy Cow! Press) and *To the Disappearance* (Mongrel Empire Press). Recent work has been anthologized in *Bull Buffalo and Indian Paintbrush* (the Poetry of Oklahoma), the *Beat Generation Anthology, Release Me, the Spirits of Greenwood Speak,* and *The Eloquent Poem.*

Matthew Guenette makes a killer breakfast: fried eggs over hash browns with hot sauce. He is the author of three full-length poetry collections: *Vasectomania* (U of Akron Press, 2017), *American Busboy* (U of Akron Press, 2011), and *Sudden Anthem* (Dream Horse Press, 2008). He received his MFA in Creative Writing from Southern Illinois University, and his BA in English from the University of New Hampshire. He still dreams of that one time he dunked. He teaches composition and creative writing at Madison College and lives in Madison, Wisconsin, with his wife, their two children, and a 20-pound cat named Butternut.

Ken Hada has a new collection of poetry, *Contour Feathers,* (Turning Plow Pres), coming out in fall 2021. His two latest books are: *Sunlight & Cedar* and *Not Quite Pilgrims* (Chicago: VACPoetry,

2020 & 2019). Ken's work has been awarded by the National Western Heritage Museum, SCMLA, Western Writers of America, Oklahoma Center for the Book and the NPR program, *The Writer's Almanac*. Ken teaches at East Central University where he has directed the annual Scissortail Creative Writing Festival for 17 years. More information is available at kenhada.org.

Carol Hamilton is retired from teaching 2nd grade through graduate school in Connecticut, Indiana, and Oklahoma, storytelling and medical translating. She is a former Poet Laureate of Oklahoma and has published 17 books: children's novels, legends and poetry and has been nominated nine times for a Pushcart Prize. She has won a Southwest Book Award, Oklahoma Book Award, David Ray Poetry Prize, *Byline Magazine*-literary awards in both short story and poetry, Warren Keith Poetry Award, Pegasus Award, and a *Chiron Review* Chapbook Award.

Michelle Hartman is the author of four books available on Amazon, along with three chapbooks. Hartman's work can be found online, in multiple journals in America and various countries overseas. She is the former editor of *Red River Review* and co-owner of the Hungry Buzzard Press.

Joseph Harrington is the author of *Of Some Sky* (BlazeVOX 2018); *Goodnight Whoever's Listening* (Essay Press 2015); *Things Come On* (an amneoir) (Wesleyan 2011); and the critical work *Poetry and the Public* (Wesleyan 2002). His creative work has appeared in *BAX: The Best American Experimental Writing 2016, Colorado Review, The Rumpus, Hotel America, Tupelo Quarterly*, and elsewhere. He teaches at the University of Kansas.

Allison Adelle Hedge Coke, poet or something. Here, considering life along I35 on the east side of Blind Lemon Road intersection with South Sooner and parallel to it on Indian Meridian Road just above Coffee Creek, where she gathered patience from Sister & Spirit her Medicine Hat and Frost Buckskin mustangs, tree frogs in summer, nights under massive amounts of stars, migrating ants, tarantulas, snakes, and birds, and where bones never lie.

Crag Hill is co-editor of *Level Land* and many other books. He is also full professor in the College of Education at the University of

Oklahoma. His two, single-author books are *Dict.* (Xexoxial Editions, 1982/2008) and *7 x 7* (Otoliths, 2010). He is co-author or co-editor on a number of scholarly, critical, and creative texts, including *Critical Explorations of Canonical Young Adult Literature: Identifying and Critiquing the Canon* (Routledge, 2020); *Critical Approaches to Teaching the High School Novel: Reinterpreting Canonical Literature* (Routledge, 2018); *Teaching Comics Through Multiple Lenses: Critical Perspectives* (Routledge, 2016); *The Critical Merits of Young Adult Literature: Coming of Age* (Routledge, 2014).

Sy Hoahwah (Yapai Nʉʉ/Kwaharʉ/Southern Arapaho) is an enrolled member of the Comanche Nation of Oklahoma. He received his M.F.A. in Creative Writing from the University of Arkansas. Hoawah is the author of three collections of poetry, *Ancestral Demon of a Grieving Bride* (University of New Mexico Press, 2021), *Night Cradle* (USPOCO Books, 2011), and *Velroy and the Madischie Mafia* (West End Press, 2009). In 2013, Sy was a recipient of the National Endowment for the Arts Literature Fellowship.

A. H. Hofer is from the Whitewater Valley of Eastern Indiana. He studied Creative Writing at Indiana State University and Wichita State University, where he earned his MFA. He has taught English at several colleges around the U.S. and teaches currently at Ivy Tech Community College in Indianapolis. Hofer's work has most recently appeared in *Willows Wept Review, Ascent Aspirations, Barrier Islands Review,* and *Assisi.*

LeAnne Howe and Dean Rader have, between them, authored, edited, or co-edited, nearly 20 books and are on the Oklahoma Republican Party's 10 Most Wanted List. In fact, they are prohibited from entering the state of Oklahoma until they rewrite all of their books making everything rhyme or about cowboys. Or Reba McEntire.

Ann Howells edited *Illya's Honey* for nineteen years—both in print and online. Her latest books are *So Long As We Speak Their Names* (Kelsay Books, 2019) and *Painting the Pinwheel Sky* (Assure Press, 2020). Two of her chapbooks were published through contests: *Black Crow in Flight* (Main Street Rag Publishing, 2007) and *Softly Beating Wings* (William D. Barney Competition/Blackbead Books,

2017). She is a multiple Pushcart nominee whose work appears in many small press and university journals.

Jack J. B. Hutchens was born and raised among the Flint Hills of Kansas. He attended Emporia State University where he studied poetry under Phil Heldrich and Christopher Howell. After graduation, he lived in Poland for several years, finding a new home there. When he returned, he completed his PhD in Slavic Literatures at the University of Illinois Urbana-Champaign. He now teaches Polish literature at Loyola University Chicago, and lives in Champaign with his wife Amanda, and their daughter Harriet. He is the author of a book of poetry, *There/Here: Poems of Journey and Home*, and a monograph *Queer Transgressions in Twentieth-Century Polish Fiction*.

Jessica Isaacs is the founder and co-editor of *Dragon Poet Review*, an online literary journal. Her book, *Deep August* (Village Books Press), received the 2015 Oklahoma Book Award for Poetry. Her poems appear in various publications, most recently including *Oklahoma Today, The Ekphrastic Review, Oklahoma Humanities* (online), *Ain't Gonna Be Treated This Way, Poetry Bay, Mothers Always Write, One Sentence Poems*, and *Malpais Review*. She teaches writing and humanities courses at Seminole State College in Oklahoma.

JL Jacobs, MFA, Brown University, is the author of four volumes of poetry. Work has appeared in numerous journals including *Ploughshares, New American Writing, Ariel Chart, Maple Tree Literary Supplement, New Orleans Review, Poetry Pacifica* and *Le Spectre Politerary Journal*. Representative work is anthologized in *American Poetry: The Next Generation*, Carnegie Mellon UP. She was a 2017 nominee for Poet Laureate of Oklahoma. She studied with C.D. Wright, John Yau, and Keith Waldrop at Brown, and has continued a mixed-media artist practice from teaching Poetry & Image at Brown Learning Community to offering mixed-media workshops at OKC Literary Festivals. She serves as editor of Pushcart Award winning journal *Abstract Magazine: Contemporary Expressions*.

Catherine Katey Johnson is an award-winning author, a Woody Guthrie Poet and BEAT Poet whose works are included in films, books, anthologies, literary journals, and chapbooks in many works such as *Poets to Come,* Walt Whitman's Bicentennial Anthology, *BEAT-itude* and *We Are BEAT. Fifty Shades of Gray Hair, a tangled collection,* and *Resting Soil* are her latest poetry collections. She has earned degrees from Rose State College and the University of Central Oklahoma. Born an Okie, her family is listed among the First Families of the Territory.

Megan Kaminski is a poet and essayist—and the author of three books of poetry, *Gentlewomen* (Noemi, 2020), *Deep City* (Noemi Press, 2015) and *Desiring Map* (Coconut Books, 2012). *Prairie Divination,* her forthcoming illustrated collection of essays + oracle deck with artist L. Ann Wheeler, turns to the plants, animals, and geological features of the prairie ecosystem as guides for living in good relation to each other—and to re-aligning thinking towards kinship, community, and interdependence. An Associate Professor in English and Co-Director of the Global Grasslands CoLABorative at the University of Kansas, she specializes in poetry and poetics, plant studies, queer ecology, somatics, eco-arts practices, and the environmental humanities. Her work is informed by interdisciplinary research in social welfare, evolutionary biology, and philosophy, as well as previous work in the healing arts and at non-profit environmental organizations.

Ashley Smith Keyfitz (Ash Smith) is the author of *Water Shed, Come Such Frequency, Pigeon of Tears, & Park of Unwired Asking* (forthcoming). Formerly a publisher for LRL magazine & book series, she lives in Austin, Texas where she does web design, graphic design, and community outreach work.

Stacy Kidd is a writer from Stillwater, Oklahoma. Her poems have appeared recently in *Berkeley Poetry Review, The Cincinnati Review, The Illanot Review,* and *Salt Hill.*

Ted Kooser, a former US Poet Laureate and Pulitzer winner, grew up in Ames, Iowa, and the next town to the east was Nevada. I35 runs between those two communities. The setting of his poem, "A Reappearance," is about six miles from I35.

Quraysh Ali Lansana is author of twenty books in poetry, nonfiction and children's literature. Lansana is a Tulsa Artist Fellow, Writer in Residence and Adjunct Professor at Oklahoma State University-Tulsa, and a former faculty member of the School of the Art Institute of Chicago, and The Juilliard School. Lansana is executive producer of KOSU/NPR's *Focus: Black Oklahoma*. His most recent books include *Opal's Greenwood Oasis, the skin of dreams: new and collected poems, 1995-2018, The Whiskey of Our Discontent: Gwendolyn Brooks as Conscience & Change Agent* (Haymarket Books, 2017) and *The BreakBeat Poets: New American Poetry in the Age of Hip Hop* (Haymarket Books, 2015). Lansana's work appears in *Best American Poetry 2019*, and and his forthcoming titles include *Those Who Stayed: Life in 1921 Tulsa After the Massacre*. He is a founding member of Tri-City Collective.

Catherine A. Lee began exploring poetry as a percussive voice with jazz musicians at a loft space/nonprofit she founded and ran in Boston (1978). These days, from San Antonio TX, and Asheville NC, Lee writes, sits in "on poem" at jam sessions, reads at open poetry events, and creates multimedia poetry pieces archived on Soundcloud (http://soundcloud.com/jazz-cat-lee) and Vimeo (http://vimeo.com/jazzovation). Lee also blogs about notable musical/poetic collaborations on her Facebook page, Jazz Ovation Inn, and has produced several artist handmade, signed, numbered, limited edition chapbooks augmented with music.

Lisa Lewis published six books of poetry, most recently *The Body Double* (Georgetown Review Press, 2015) and *Taxonomy of the Missing* (The Word Works, 2018). She also has a new chapbook, *The Borrowing Days* (Ermys Press, 2021). Her work has appeared in dozens of literary magazines since 1983, including *Poetry, American Poetry Review, Kenyon Review, Fence, New England Review*, and *Missouri Review*. She teaches in the creative writing program at Oklahoma State University, which she directed from 2000 to 2016.

Adrian Louis (Lovelock Paiute) (1946-2018) considered himself a "poet for the downtrodden," and often wrote survivalist poetry. His 19 collections won him acclaim and a wide readership. In addition, his novel, *Skins* (1995), was adapted into a film, which premiered at Sundance. He was the eldest of 12 children. He co-founded the Native American Journalists Association.

Denise Low, Ph.D., is a former Poet Laureate of Kansas and winner of the Red Mountain Press Editor's Choice Award, among other honors. She has taught creative writing at the University of Richmond and the University of Kansas, and she founded the creative writing program at Haskell Indian Nations University, where she taught 25 years. She now teaches for Baker University. Her memoir *The Turtle's Beating Heart: One Family's Story of Lenape Survival* is from the University of Nebraska Press.

J. C Mahan / Johnie Catfish is a street poet in awe of academics and in spite of conventions offering a variety of poetry from form to very free verse unapologetically on any subject that comes to mind. He is a lover of people and words. He longs for a conversation with you.

Jeff Martin is an author, editor, Chapter Leader for PEN America Tulsa, and President/Co-Founder of the nonprofit Magic City Books.

Sharon Edge Martin has published in Alfred Hitchcock's *Mystery Magazine, Family Circle, Oklahoma Today, Outside, True West,* and other publications. Her work is included in Michael Bugeja's *The Art and Craft of Poetry* and in *Poet's Market* from Writer's Digest Books. She writes for Oklahoma Observer and hosts a monthly poetry reading at Tidewater Winery in rural Oklahoma. She has two books from Village Books Press, *Not a Prodigal* (2018), and I've *Got the Blues: Looking for Justice in a Red State* (2019). She is currently at work on a novel in verse.

Jim McCrary lives in Lawrence, Kansas within sight of Oregon, Santa Fe and California trails. His latest work appears in *Ha(Na) Ka* anthology and *End of the World* anthology. *Red Hot Son Ette* published by Really Old Gringo Press and *Year Book* from Shirt Pocket Press.

Patricia L. Meek won AWP Intro for Fiction, "The Crucified Bird," and "Weather" was a 2016 finalist for Rita Dove Award in Poetry. Her writing has recently appeared in *The Hong Kong Review, Ghost Town Literary Journal, Penman Review.* Her poetry video series, Dialogue with Georgia O'Keefe, has been showcased at Rabbit Heart Poetry film festival and the Santa Fe Film Festival. Author of *NOAH: a supernatural eco-thriller,* published by All Things That Matter Press. She holds a BA in Creative Writing from Louisiana State University, an MFA in Creative Writing from Wichita State University, and an MA in Counseling from Southwestern College in Santa Fe, New Mexico. She is currently an Outpatient Clinician (LPC) in Southern Colorado, United States. Website: www.patricialmeek.com.

Jeanetta Calhoun Mish's books are *What I Learned at the War,* a poetry collection (West End Press, 2016) and *Oklahomeland:*

Essays (Lamar University Press, 2015). Her 2009 poetry collection, *Work Is Love Made Visible* (West End Press) won an Oklahoma Book Award, a Wrangler Award, and the WILLA Award from Women Writing the West. Dr. Mish teaches for The Red Earth Creative Writing MFA at Oklahoma City University. She served as Oklahoma State Poet Laureate from 2017-2020; in 2019, she was awarded a Poets Laureate Fellowship from the Academy of American Poets.

Lisa Moore's poems have appeared in *Nimrod International Journal, Borderlands Texas Poetry Review,* and *Sinister Wisdom,* among other venues. Her chapbook *24 HOURS OF MEN* was published by Dancing Girl Press in 2018. A Lambda-Award-winning critic, Lisa is Archibald A. Hill Professor of English and Director of LGBTQ Studies at The University of Texas at Austin.

Desiree Morales is a poet and educator living in Los Angeles, California. Her work has appeared in *What Rough Beast, Conflict of Interest,* and the *I Scream Social Anthology.* She lived in Austin, Texas for ten years and plans to never stop talking about it.

Benjamin Myers is a former Poet Laureate of Oklahoma and the author of three books of poetry, *Elegy for Trains* (Village Books Press), *Lapse Americana* (New York Quarterly Books), and *Black Sunday: The Dust Bowl Sonnets* (Lamar University Literary Press). His poems have appeared in *Image, Ninth Letter, The Yale Review,* and other journals. He is the Crouch-Mathis Professor of Literature at Oklahoma Baptist University, and has written about poetry for *World Literature Today, Oklahoma Today,* and other publications.

Brent Newsom received the Maureen Egen Writers Exchange Award in poetry from Poets & Writers, and has also won the Foley Poetry Prize from America. He wrote the libretto for *A Porcelain Doll,* an opera based on the life of deaf-blind pioneer Laura Bridgman, and is the author of *Love's Labors* (CavanKerry Press, 2015), which was a finalist for the Oklahoma Book Award in poetry. His poems have also appeared in *Southern Review, Hopkins Review, Windhover, Cave Wall,* and other journals.

Eugene "Gene" Novogrodsky has lived in Brownsville, Texas, for 33 years. He writes slices of the Texas-Mexican border. He is a founding member of the bi-lingual Narciso Martinez Cultural Arts

Center Writers Form in San Benito, Texas, now in its third decade. He taught various writing, reading and language courses at the University of Texas-Brownsville. He is an economic and environmental sustainability advocate. He is a member of several book clubs, and also a local ad hoc writers' group. Partner Ruth E. Wagner has encouraged all his writing, reading, and political activities.

Shin Yu Pai is a poet, essayist and visual artist. She is the author of several books of poetry, including *ENSŌ* (Entre Ríos Books, 2020), *SIGHTINGS: SELECTED WORKS (2000-2005)* (1913 Press, 2007), *AUX ARCS* (La Alameda, 2013), *Adamantine* (White Pine, 2010), and *Equivalence* (La Alameda, 2003). She served as the fourth poet laureate of the city of Redmond from 2015 to 2017 and has been an artist in residence for the Seattle Art Museum, Town Hall Seattle, and Pacific Science Center. In 2014, she was nominated for a Stranger Genius Award in Literature. She is a three-time fellow of MacDowell and has also been in residence at Taipei Artist Village, Soul Mountain, The Ragdale Foundation, Centrum, and The National Park Service. Her poetry films have screened at the Zebra Poetry Festival and the Northwest Film Forum's Cadence video poetry festival. She currently lives and works in the Pacific Northwest.

Gus Palmer, Jr. (pànthai:dê 'White Cloud') is member of the Kiowa tribe and professor emeritus in linguistic anthropology from the University of Oklahoma. He has published two books, *Telling Stories the Kiowa Way* (2003) and *When Dream Bear Sings* (2018). In addition to language work in his native Kiowa, he has published poems and stories in anthologies and literary magazines. He worked with son, filmmaker Jeffrey Palmer, on the 2018 PBS American Masters documentary film, "N. Scott Momaday: Words from a Bear."

Dave Parsons, 2011 Texas State Poet Laureate, has published seven collections of poetry, his latest are *Reaching For Longer Water, Selected & New Poems* and *Far Out: Poems of the 60's* (co-edited with Wendy Barker). Parsons was inducted into the Texas Institute of Letters in 2009. He has taught English at Lone Star College since 1992 and also teaches creative writing at the University of St. Thomas. He lives in Conroe, Texas, with his wife, Nancy, an award-winning artist.

Jason Poudrier is a 2018 Pat Tillman Scholar and graduate of the Red Earth MFA Program at Oklahoma City University. He is an award-winning writer and Purple Heart recipient of the Iraq War, currently pursuing a Ph.D. in English Education at the University of Oklahoma. He also serves as the arts and humanities administrator for Lawton, Oklahoma. His poetry collection *Red Fields* was published by Mongrel Empire Press in 2012.

Kevin Prufer's eighth book of poems is *The Art of Fiction: Poems,* published by Four Way Books. His previous collection, *How He Loved Them,* was long-listed for the 2019 Pulitzer Prize and received the Julie Suk Award for the best book of poems from the American literary press. He teaches in the creative writing program at The University of Houston.

Marcie Rendon, citizen of the White Earth Nation. She was listed in Oprah Magazine's 2020 list of 31 Native American Author's to read. 2020 McKnight Distinguished Artist Award and 50 over 50 MN AARP & Pollen Award. Rendon's novel *Girl Gone Missing* is the second Cash Blackbear novel and was nominated for the Putnam's Son's Sue Grafton Memorial Award at the Edgars, 2020. *Murder on the Red River* (2017 Cinco Puntos Press) received the Pinckley Women's Debut Crime Novel Award 2018 and the Western Writers of America Spur Award Finalist 2018 Contemporary Novel category. Rendon has non-fiction children's books and four plays published. Her script, *Sweet Revenge,* was chosen to be performed as a staged reading in the Oklahoma Indigenous Theatre Company's 2020 New Native American Play Festival. The creative mind of Raving Native Theater, she curated Twin Cities Public Television's *Art Is...Creative Native Resilience 2019.* Diego Vazquez and Rendon received the Loft's 2017 Spoken Word Immersion Fellowship for work with incarcerated women.

Lydia Renfro holds an MFA from Adelphi University and is the recipient of the Donald Everett Axinn Award for Fiction. Her work has appeared in *Litro Magazine, Siblini Journal, The Blue Nib, Witches Mag, WordCity Monthly, Miletus International Literature Magazine, Isacoustic,* and others. She is the current fiction editor at *The Blue Nib* and lives in Colorado.

C. R. Resetarits has had work recently in *North Dakota Review, Southern Humanities Review*, and *Native Voices: Indigenous American Poetry, Craft and Conversations* (Tupelo Press). New work is in *Confrontation, Hobart, The Chicago Review*, and *Yellow Medicine Review*. She lives in Faulkner-riddled Oxford, Mississippi.

MW Rishell lives a quiet life in Mesa, Arizona, and bothers no one while longing to return to I35.

W. Jackson Rushing III is Professor Emeritus of Visual Arts at the University of Oklahoma, who knows I35 from Laredo to OKC like the back of his hand. A former Fellow of the Guggenheim Foundation, his poems have been published in *Analecta, River Styx,* and *Borderlands: The Texas Poetry Review.*

Siobhan Scarry is the author of *Pilgrimly* (Parlor Press / Free Verse Editions, 2014). Her creative work has appeared or is forthcoming in *The Cincinnati Review, Colorado Review, jubilat, Mid-American Review, New Letters,* and *Terrain,* among others. She also publishes scholarly work on 20th-21st century poetries, with recent work appearing in *Paideuma* and *Southern Humanities Review.* In 2021, she was awarded a fellowship from the Nancy B. Negley Artists Residency Foundation at the Dora Maar House in France. She is currently Associate Professor at Bethel College in Kansas, where she teaches literature and creative writing, runs a visiting writers series, and serves as faculty mentor to the undergraduate literary magazine *YAWP!*

Kyle Schlesinger is a poet and critic living in Austin. Recent books include *Swish Void* (a collaboration with Grant Cross, Great Fainting Spell, 2018), *Let's Drift* (c_L Books, 2017), and *Life,* a collaboration with Ted Greenwald, from Kin Press.

Jan Seale, the 2012 Texas Poet Laureate, lives in McAllen, Texas. Her poems and prose have been published widely, her latest books being *A Lifetime of Words,* a collection of essays (2020), and *Particulars: poems of smallness* (2021), both published by Lamar University Literary Press. She has held a National Endowment for the Arts Fellowship in Poetry and is a member of the Texas Institute of Letters.

John Selvidge's poetry has appeared in publications such as *BlazeVOX, Otoliths, Nerve Lantern, Gauss PDF, Creative Thresholds, Moria,* and several others, both under his own name and as a member of the experimental poetry collectives j4 and the Atlanta Poets Group, for whose 2012 anthology *The Lattice Inside* he served as a co-editor. He has lived in Colorado, New Orleans, the Washington D.C. area, and Atlanta, where he pursued a doctorate in comparative literature at Emory. He currently lives in Oklahoma City, his hometown, where he works in the humanitarian nonprofit sector, as a freelance arts and culture writer, and in the local film scene as screenwriter, actor, and producer.

Steven B. Sexton (Choctaw / Pawnee) is an assistant professor at the University of Nevada, Las Vegas, where he is teaching American and Native American literature. His approach to literature, in both the classroom and his scholarship, is to view them as stories. He likes the kinds of stories poetry opens up.

Former teaching artist, Sandra Soli is a writer and copy editor in Edmond, OK. She has published poetry, short fiction, articles, and photographs for four decades. A long-time poet in Woody Guthrie and Scissortail festivals, she authored two poetry chapbooks, sponsored anthologies and readings to benefit food pantries, and served on the board of Oklahoma's Center for the Book. Honors include Pushcart nominations, a *Highlights for Children* magazine prize, and an Oklahoma Book Award.

Tony Spicer grew up in a swath of Oklahoma and Arkansas stretching from Memphis to Oklahoma City. His poems have appeared in *Crazy Horse* and *Cream City Review,* among others. He lives and teaches in Ypsilanti, Michigan.

Gregory Stapp received his BA in Creative Writing from the University of Oklahoma and his MFA from Queens University of Charlotte. His poems have appeared or are pending publication with *Broadsided Press, The Ekphrastic Review, Forage, The Cortland Review, The Sierra Nevada Review*, and *The Southern Review,* among others. He is currently Editor-in-Chief at *Harbor Review.*

Don Stinson lives in Tonkawa, OK, and teaches at Northern Oklahoma College, where he also organizes the annual Chikaskia Literary Festival. He is the author of two poetry collections, *Flatline Horizon*

(Mongrel EMpire Press, 2018) and *Hunger* (TURNing Plow Press, 2020), which was a finalist for the 2021 Oklahoma Book Award. He has published widely in regional and online journals and has been a featured reader at venues throughout Oklahoma. He studied creative writing at Oklahoma State University, where he received a Ph.D. in English.

Jane Taylor lives in Oklahoma City and teaches creative writing at Ghost Ranch in New Mexico, and occasionally does workshops locally. She has an MA in English/creative writing from UCO. Her most recent book of poetry, *Pencil Light*, was published by Turning Point Press (WordTech.) You can see more about her teaching and writing life at www.janevincenttaylor.blogspot.com.

William Trowbridge's eighth poetry collection is *Oldguy: Superhero— The Complete Collection*, Red Hen Press, 2019. His ninth, *Call Me Fool*, is forthcoming from Red Hen in 2022. He is a faculty mentor in the University of Nebraska Omaha Low-residency MFA in Writing Program and was Poet Laureate of Missouri from 2012 to 2016.

Loretta Diane Walker, a member of the Texas Institute of Letters,was a Best of the Net Nominee and a nine-time Pushcart Nominee, won the 2021 William D. Barney Memorial Chapbook Contest sponsored by the Fort Worth Poetry Society, the 2016 Phyllis Wheatley Book Award and the 2011 Bluelight Press Book Award. Her work has appeared in various literary journals, magazines, and anthologies throughout the United States, Canada, India, Ireland, and the UK. She has published five collections of poetry. Both her chapbook, *From the Cow's Eye and Other Poems* and her full-length manuscript, *Day Begins When Darkness is In Full Bloom,* Bluelight Press, were released in 2021. She taught music in Odessa, Texas.

Ron Wallace is an Oklahoma native and currently an adjunct instructor of English at Southeastern Oklahoma State University, in Durant, Oklahoma, where he was born and raised. His father served as a police officer there, rising to the rank of captain. He is the author of ten books of poetry, five of which have been finalists in the Oklahoma Book Awards. *Renegade and Other Poems* was the 2018 winner of the Oklahoma Book Award. His last book, *The Last Blue Sky* was his fifth finalist. Wallace has been a Pushcart Prize nominee and the winner of the 2017 Songs of Eretz Poetry Award. He has recently been published in *Oklahoma Today, Red River Review, San Pedro River Review, Concho River Review, Red Earth Review,*

Oklahoma Humanities Magazine, Borderlands, and a number of other magazines and journals. He has also just edited *Bull Buffalo and Indian Paintbrush, a Collection of Oklahoma Poetry.*

Josh Wann is an educator and storyteller who lives in Tulsa, Oklahoma with his wife and hoard of children. He's available for a variety of creative gigs at wannjt@gmail.com. He has been published in *Concis, Hard Crackers, Calliope Crashes, Dragon Poet Review,* and *Sugar Mule,* among others. He believes in climbing trees and coffee and pie.

Scott Weaver's poems have appeared in *Rattle, The New York Quarterly, DIAGRAM, UCity Review,* and other journals. His first collection, *Home & Ghost,* is available from Urban Farmhouse Press. Scott earned his MFA in creative writing from George Mason University, where he was a Heritage Fellow. He lives with his wife, Kelli Jo Fod, and their daughter, Cypress, in Richmond, Virginia, and teaches English at Reynolds Community College. Find him here: http://www.scott-weaver.com.

Cullen Whisenhunt is a graduate of Oklahoma City University's Red Earth Creative Writing MFA program. His work has been included in *Atlas Poetica 40, Frogpond, Ninth Letter, The Ekphrastic Review,* and *Dragon Poet Review,* among other publications. He was the featured poet for *Red River Review*'s August 2019 issue, and his work was also included in the anthology *Bull Buffalo and Indian Paintbrush: Poetry of Oklahoma.*

Logan Mikal White-Mulcare is an Oklahoma poet, abstract painter, mixed media artist, and writer of short fiction and essays. He isn't well known for these things, but he does them often and very few people have told him to quit. Logan is a citizen of the Cherokee Nation. His art may not always explore heritage directly, but he sees his works as purposeful acts of survivance, each piece or poem adding to the greater collective of modern Indigenous American expression, which he understands to be a living and evolving thing.

Now retired in Norman OK, J.D. Whitney taught composition & literature for many years for the University of Wisconsin Colleges (Wausau) and College of Menominee Nation (Keshena, WI). He's had poetry published in many periodicals (*Poetry, Orion, Runes, Origin, Beloit Poetry Journal, Caterpillar, El Corno Emplumado,* etc.)

and fellowships from the Wisconsin Arts Board and the National Endowment for the Arts. His books include *The Nabisco Warehouse, SD, Grandmother Says, All My Relations* (books 1 and 2), and *Sweeping the Broom Shorter* (his selected poems from *Longhouse,* 2014).

W. L. Winter views bios as Borges considered mirrors, as a little untrustworthy, and leaks into another dimension. He studied political science at Sierra College in northern California, and creative writing in Tulsa, Oklahoma. His poetry skills were honed on the streets of San Francisco and on Route 66 between Oklahoma and California. He reads regularly and is an occasional host at Full Circle Last Sunday Poetry reading in Oklahoma City.

Ricco Wright is the managing editor of *The Black Wall Street Times,* the poetry editor of *Calliope Crashes,* and a *2018 Woody Guthrie Poet.* He also has written for *NewBlackMan (in Exile), The Langston Gazette* and *TC Today,* and has been a featured commentator on NPR, CNN Live, and CNN International. A Bill Gates Scholar from 2000 to 2010, Wright received his bachelor's degree in mathematics from Langston University and his doctoral degree in mathematics education from Teachers College, Columbia University. He has taught mathematics at the Borough of Manhattan Community College, the Fashion Institute of Technology, and Langston University. He currently lives in New York City and has two daughters, Raquel and Raya.

Rebecca Zweig's work has been featured in the *Boston Review, the Nation,* and the *New York Times,* among other publications. She recently held a Teaching-Writing Fellowship at the Iowa Writers' Workshop, where she won the 2018 Prairie Lights / Donald Justice Prize for Poetry. She is currently a Visiting Assistant Professor at the University of Iowa.

Acknowledgements

Alyan, "Turnpike // Ghost," *The Twenty-Ninth Year,* Ecco, 2019

Alyan, "1999," *The Twenty-Ninth Year*, Ecco, 2019

Andrea Alzati, "No Hay Un Rio," *Todos mis quchillos*, Komorebi ediciones, 2019

Austin, "Portrait," *Notes On Hard Times*, Village Books Press, 2019

Bargen, "House of Turtle," *The Body of Water*, Timberline, 2003

Bargen, "Good Place to Begin," *The Body of Water,* Timberline Press, 2003

Bargen, "Abject Impermanence in Kansas," *Begin Again: 150 Kansas Poems,* Woodley Memorial Press, 2011

Bargen, "3 Chain of Being," *The Cape Rock*, 2012

Barnes, "The Last Chance," *The American Book of the Dead*, University of Illinois Press, 1982

Barnes, "Touching the Rattlesnake," *La Plata Cantata.* Purdue University Press, 1989

Barnes, "After the Great Plain," *The Sawdust War*, University of Illinois Press, 1992

Beckemeyer, "Sandhill Seasons," *Stage Whispers*, Meadowlark Books, 2018

Beckemeyer, "The Intrinsic Essence of Hay," *The Midwest Quarterly,* 2016

Beckemeyer, "Horizons," *The Ekphrastic Review*, 2017

Blaeser, "Slippage," *Copper Yearning,* Holy Cow! Press, 2019

Blaeser, "The Ritual of Washing Hands," *Copper Yearning*, Holy Cow! Press, 2019

Bond, "Lakes of the Southern Plains," *North American Review*, 2017

Bond, "The Stones of April," *Cimarron Review*, 2017

Bowers, "An Oklahoma Weather Poem that Makes No Mention of Tornadoes," *Occasional Hymns*, Turning Plow Press, 2018

Bowers, "I Shalopy Moo," *Occasional Hymns*, Turning Plow Press, 2018

Boyden, "What We Did Instead," *Writing for Peace*, 2013

Bradford, "Transformers," Truck, *I35 Creativity Corridor,* http://halvard-johnson.blogspot.com

Bradford, "Triweekly Cimarron River Report, May 17th to August 28th," *Nomads with Samsonite*, BlazeVOX, 2011

Brown, R., "Drops in the Funnel," *Welcome to FOB Haiku: War Poems from Inside the Wire,* 2015

Brown, R., "Fighting Seasons," *Midwestern Gothic*, Summer 2015

Castillo, "Wetback," *Gulf Coast: A Journal of Literature and Fine Arts,* 2016

Castillo, "Immigration interview with Don Francisco," *PBS Newshour*, 2016

Castillo, "Immigration interview with Jay Leno," *Cenzontle*, BOA Limited Editions, 2014

Castleberry, "Errors of the Sun," *Trajectory*, 2019

Castleberry, "The House of Hours," *In Between Hangovers*, 2016

Chandler, "Sawhorse," *Hugging This Rock*, Middle West Press, 2017

Clewell, "Sonata for Tornado in EF-5 (Major): May 22, 2011, 5:41-6:13pm," *Almost Nothing To Be Scared Of*, U of Wisconsin P, 2016

Da', "Earth Mover," Tributaries, University of Arizona Press, 2015

Hada, "Margaritas and Redfish," *Margaritas and Redfish*, Lamar University Press, 2013

Hamilton, "Space," *The Midwest Quarterly*, 1999

Hamilton, "Through the Arbuckles," *The Midwest Quarterly*, 2000

Hartman, "Wormwood," *Free State Review*, 2018

Hartman, "They Say the Journey Is Everything," *Better Than Starbucks*, July 2018

Hoahwah, "Comancheria," *Velroy and the Madischie Mafia*, West End Press, 2009

Howells, "J'eat yet?" *Poetry at Round Top*, 2011

Isaacs, "Tender of Flesh," *Deep August*, Village Books Press, 2014

Johnson, "Moments after Murrah," *Fifty Shades of Gray Hair*, KariGrant Press, 2018

Kaminski, "Wintering Prairies," Truck, *I35 Creativity Corridor*, http://halvard-johnson.blogspot.com

Kidd, "This Is One of the Nine Wide Worlds, and the Creatures that Inhabit it Lull," *The Iowa Review*, 2009

Kidd, "bark," *Phoebe*, 2014

Lansana, "Will Rogers Turnpike," *Walmart Republic*, Mongrel Empire Press, 2014

Lee, "Texas Road Trip," *Voices de la Luna*, February 2018

Louis, "Electric Snakes," *Electric Snakes*, The Backwaters Press, 2018

Louis, "Skinology," *Electric Snakes*, The Backwaters Press, 2018

Louis, "The Motherland," *Electric Snakes*, The Backwaters Press, 2018

Low, "Weep Willow," *Shadow Light: Poems*, Red Mountain Press, 2018

Low, "Stomp Dance: Wyandotte County," *Shadow Light: Poems*, Red Mountain Press, 2018

Low, "Chicory Afternoon," *Shadow Light: Poems*, Red Mountain Press, 2018

Meek, "Weather," *Natural Bridge, A Journal of Contemporary Literature*, 2017

Mish, "Rio de los Carneros Cimarron," *New Plains Review*, 2017

Desiree Morales, "Calpurnia in Tejas," Indolent Books, *What Rough Beast* (series), 2018

Myers, "After the Grass Fires," *Poetry Northwest*, 2009

Myers, "What to Do After a Tornado," *The Yale Review*, 2014

Newsom, "Horticulture," *Love's Labors,* CavanKerry Press, 2015

Novogrodsky, "Cool Tiles," https://writersoftheriogrande.com

Pai, "Inner Space," *AUX ARCS*, La Alameda Press, 2013

Palmer, "Incident at Cornfields," *Construction Literary Magazine*, 2015

Parsons, "Color of Mourning," *Louisiana Literature,* 2003

Parsons, "Ghost Hawk," *The Texas Review,* 2014

Parsons, "Knowing Texas," *The World Keeps Turning to Light: A Renga by the State Poets Laureate of America,* Negative Capability Press, 2013

Poudrier, "Dream Song Delta 1-39," *World Literature Today*, 2013

Kevin Prufer, 4-Way Books

Resetarits, "Ocotillo," *Manifest West: Weird West, Western Press Books,* 2015

Scarry, "Jubilate," Sentence: A Journal of Prose Poetics, 2013

Scarry, "Old 81," *Truck, I35 Creativity Corridor*, http://halvard-johnson.blogspot.com, 2015

Seale, "Traveling North: The Rules," *The Wonder Is*, 2nd ed., Ink Brush Press, 2012

Stapp, "Legend," *Eunoia Review,* 2012

Stinson, "Prairie Metaphysics," *The Midland Review*

Trowbridge, "Interstate," *O Paradise,* University of Arkansas Press, 1995

Trowbridge, "The Road," *Put This On, Please: New and Selected Poems,* Red Hen Press, 2014

Walker, "Bruised," *Red River Review,* 2011

Walker, "Offsprings of Extremes" *Red River Review,* 2016

Wallace, "Between the Moon and Mexico," *Cowboys and Cantos,* TJMF Publishing, 2013

Whisenhunt, "Knee Deep in October," *Among the Trees*, Fine Dog Press, 2021

Wright, "Native American Day," *Calliope Crashes,* 2018

In memoriam . . . a moment of silence:

As *Level Land* transitioned from a multitude of submissions to an anthology, several contributors passed away—much to our sadness and dismay. They include: David Clewell (1955-2020), Adrian Louis (1946-2018), and Loretta Diane Walker (1958-2022). While we are devastated with their passing, we are much better for knowing them and their amazing work. We hope you will celebrate their lives and legacies by continuing to read their poetry and providing witness for their writing, labor, and kindness.